"*Dare to Prepare* conveys Ron's down-to-earth wisdom about the critical first step in the success cycle . . . and it has applications to every challenge we face in life, work, and relationships."
—**David Barrett**, president and CEO,
Hearst-Argyle Television, Inc.

"Ron Shapiro's emphasis on preparation is dead-on. The proven strategies he shares here, drawn from both his successful life as a businessman, sports agent, and a father, and numerous fascinating successful leaders in a variety of other industries, can help anyone be better at his or her endeavors. This book is a must-have for anyone looking to get ahead in life. Ron Shapiro has always had a lot to teach people about success in work and in life. *Dare to Prepare* might be his best guide yet."
—**Billy Beane**, general manager, Oakland Athletics,
and the subject of the bestselling book *Moneyball*

"Shapiro presents a compelling case for how eight simple steps can make you, your team, and your partners all winners—if you only have the discipline! And if that is something you're lacking, he'll show you how to overcome that, too!"
—**Liza Cartmell**, group president,
ARAMARK Sports and Entertainment

"Whether you are educating a sales force, managers, or front-line company representatives, or just looking to improve your own efficiency and success rate, this book is a great resource."
—**John Cochran**, senior executive,
Bank of America Card Services

"Using interviews with 'master preparers' and high achievers like Jets coach Eric Mangini, a heroic woman who battles wildfires, a high-powered television executive, and historian Taylor Branch, Ron Shapiro shows how their preparation secrets, properly utilized, can pave the way to success. Whether you are an entrepreneur planning to build a better mousetrap, a businessperson entering a negotiation, or a historian starting a new book, I believe that you can learn—and profit—from Ron Shapiro's winning strategies. I did."
—**Kenneth C. Davis**, *New York Times* bestselling
author of *Don't Know Much About® History*

"This book shows that leadership is not just about instinct, charisma, and rhetoric; it's even more about preparation, planning, and perspiration. We owe it to the next generation to think before we speak and to plan before we act. With the use of compelling real-life examples and anecdotes from leaders from all sectors, *Dare to Prepare* is an indispensable primer for effective decision-making and impactful action."

—**Lee Fisher**, lieutenant governor of Ohio

"The journey is the destination for Shapiro's loyal readers. In the same way that professional athletes prepare completely, this book provides the insights for business strategists to play at the top of their game. Two types exist in the business world today. Those who read Shapiro's book and heed his advice will hike their success rate in practice. And then, there are the others. . . ." —**Linda Ginzel**, clinical professor of managerial psychology, University of Chicago

"Ron Shapiro makes clear that—in any industry, in any sector, whatever the objective—there simply is no substitute for preparation. That is certainly true for educators. But it is the way this point is illustrated—with spare, precise advice from people who have learned in often-dramatic ways the age-old saw that failing to prepare is preparing to fail—that makes *Dare to Prepare* such an engaging, enjoyable, and ultimately indispensable read." —**Nancy S. Grasmick,** Maryland state superintendent of schools

"This book reflects years of experience, and of wisdom gained, through the careful preparation and resulting success of professionals in a variety of fields—from athletics to the arts. . . . Anyone who wants to be a successful negotiator, speaker, fund-raiser, or leader will find these stories both enlightening and entertaining."

—**Freeman A. Hrabowski, III**, president, University of Maryland, Baltimore County

"Once again, Ron Shapiro shares important principles drawn from the personal experiences of many about how to achieve winning results. Example after example makes it clear that more preparation, organization, and the application of a well-thought methodology will help us all be the best that we can be."

—**Susan Keating**, president and CEO, National Foundation for Credit Counseling

"Ron Shapiro has written a passionate, timely, and highly effective guide to business success endeavors. His zeal for preparation and powerful anecdotes are a formula for success. I will borrow from it shamelessly."
—**Len Kennedy**, general counsel, Sprint Nextel

"Ron has done it again; *Dare to Prepare* is an excellent and interesting read. Real-life stories emphasize how critical it is to properly prepare for any important negotiation. From sports examples to business and even hostage negotiation, Ron makes a compelling case to take the time and prepare the right way and 'win before you begin.'"
—**George Kilroy**, president and CEO, PHH Arval

"Once again, Ron Shapiro puts into focus the concepts we all think about but often do not practice. *Dare to Prepare* is the blueprint for obtaining results. Ron is the master at assembling the tools for success, organizing them in plain speak and delivering them to us so we can score. This is a must-read."
—**Randy Levine**, president, New York Yankees

"As a psychiatrist and teacher, I love this book. It does three things better than any other. It offers a thoughtful structure for thinking through a life problem to its solution. It provides stories with fascinating plots and outcomes, which make each of the steps in the structure clear and memorable. It promotes a feeling of relief through revealing to readers like me that we are not so different from everyone else in often failing to make a plan primarily because we're not sure how."
—**Dr. Paul McHugh**, Henry Phipps professor of psychiatry emeritus, Johns Hopkins University

"*Dare to Prepare* draws on Ronald Shapiro's extraordinary career as one of America's top negotiators and lawyers. Full of real-life examples, Shapiro shows how meticulous planning can raise the odds of success in business and in life."
—**Norman Pearlstine**, former managing editor, *The Wall Street Journal*, and former editor in chief, Time Inc.

"This is absolutely essential information for anyone from business leaders to business students. Ron Shapiro has done a wonderful job of immediately engaging the readers and never losing them, as he shares lessons learned about the value of preparing with deliberate purpose . . . the purpose to succeed. One only has to *Dare to Prepare* in order to stay ahead of the competition."

—**Dr. Kathy Player**, provost and chief academic officer, Grand Canyon University

"Ron Shapiro, the torch bearer for the Power of Nice, reveals with great insight another key to success, the Power of Preparation. Vivid accounts from Ron's career and the careers of an array of interesting people show convincingly that achieving positive outcomes through preparation applies to all personal interactions whether with family, friends, neighbors, or business."

—**Kurt Schmoke**, dean, Howard University School of Law, and former mayor of Baltimore

"Ron Shapiro offers the reader valuable insights and methods that have universal applications for facing the diverse challenges of life. He explains how thoughtful preparation empowers one to succeed in important personal and professional endeavors."

—**Ellen Johnson Sirleaf**, president, Republic of Liberia

"In *Dare to Prepare*, Ron Shapiro assembles compelling narratives from his broad experiences that will inspire you and provide you with practical tools to be a winning preparer, negotiator, and communicator."

—**Brendan Tuohey**, cofounder and executive director, PeacePlayers International

"Ron Shapiro provides a clear and compelling read for everyone. This book conveys the obvious but often overlooked fact that preparation is the key to success. And he makes his preparation system compelling with stories from highly successful people from all walks of life."

—**Fred Wilpon**, chairman and CEO, New York Mets, and chairman, Sterling Equities

DARE TO PREPARE

Also by Ronald M. Shapiro
(coauthored with Mark A. Jankowski with James Dale)

Bullies, Tyrants, and Impossible People

The Power of Nice—How to Negotiate
So Everyone Wins, Especially You!

DARE
TO
PREPARE

*How to Win
Before You Begin*

Ronald M. Shapiro

with Gregory Jordan

THREE RIVERS PRESS
NEW YORK

Published in the United States by Three Rivers Press, an imprint of the
Crown Publishing Group, a division of Random House, Inc., New York.
www.crownpublishing.com

Three Rivers Press and the Tugboat design are registered trademarks
of Random House, Inc.

Originally published in hardcover in the United States by Crown Business,
an imprint of the Crown Publishing Group, a division of Random House, Inc.,
New York, in 2008.

Library of Congress Cataloging-in-Publication Data

Shapiro, Ronald M.
  Dare to prepare : how to win before you begin / Ronald M. Shapiro with
Gregory Jordan.— 1st ed.
      p. cm.
  1. Business planning.   2. Strategic planning.   I. Jordan, Gregory.
II. Title.
   HD30.28.S4185 2008
   658.4'012—dc22   2007027965

ISBN 978-0-307-45180-4

Printed in the United States of America

Design by Joseph Rutt

10 9 8 7 6

First Paperback Edition

To Mark and Lori Jankowski,
for your inspiring example of how to respond to
that for which there can be little preparation.

CONTENTS

Part 2

THE PRINCIPLES

Part 3

THE BENEFITS OF PREPARATION

*Self-Confidence, Effectiveness,
and Satisfaction*

"A goal without a plan is just a wish."
—Antoine de Saint-Exupéry

INTRODUCTION

Will You Dare to Prepare?

The airplane shudders at the top of the runway and then springs forward. Your business trip is over, and you are headed home to the family for a long weekend. What's more, you have been upgraded to first class.

A flock of ducks sits on the grass and stares at the big metal bird roaring past. Your BlackBerry: off. Your laptop: in the overhead bin. No turbulence as you rise. You push your seat back and wait for the flight attendant with the kind smile to arrive with a drink.

You marvel: how do these people do it so well? The debonair captain with the slightly tilted cap strode into the cockpit a bit late. But his unhurried gait and sly smile gave you the confidence that you will barely notice a few bumps

during the flight. He got on the intercom with that Robert
Mitchum voice and gave the reassuring cliché: "Ladies and
gentlemen, it is a beautiful evening for flying."

It is a great evening for going home. The earth is fading
now as you look down. It is twilight, and the growing dis-
tance of the landscape and the flickering lights feed your
sense of escape.

Suddenly the plane growls. The hum of the engines stops
and the silence itself is loud. You are floating there for a few
seconds; everyone looks at one another; the flight atten-
dants freeze and you see fear in their eyes. The silence turns
deafening.

The plane turns on its left wing—your wing—and you
are looking ten thousand feet straight down as you drop
sideways toward the earth. You see the faces of your family
the whole way down.

The captain, it turns out, was not prepared. He and his
copilot rushed through the standardized pilot's checklist—
the Bible of preparation in the aviation industry—much too
quickly. Before takeoff, he neglected to release the plane's
elevator lock, the device on the rear wing that controls the
airplane's pitch.

Your beloved mother has been battling pneumonia for four
days. What a fighter she is! But with those white blood cells
so low she is a giant bull's-eye for the microscopic bacteria
that come her way. You are spending every night beside her
in one of those torturous hospital chairs. You are on the
lookout for anything that may bring bacteria too close for
comfort.

You wear a mask to protect her from the critters that your

own breath may spew. Each time you hear the door open, you look up to make sure the nurse or doctor has put on a mask, too. And you always double-check to make sure that whoever comes in squirts his or her hands with that alcohol solution in the dispenser on the wall. If one bacteria-filled finger touches that IV port, she's as good as gone.

You are exhausted and almost hallucinating. You are so tired that sometimes even you almost forget to wash your hands before you help her move her legs or adjust her pillow.

You rest your head against the back of the chair and watch her breathe. She is improving slowly. Smiling a bit again. The door opens and the night nurse carries in another IV bag. He is a fast mover: he talks fast, walks fast, and checks her temperature fast.

He is right beside her IV stand when you realize: he did not prepare properly by squirting his hands! He is reaching for the port on her arm and you almost dive across your mother on the bed to grab his hands.

You stand there holding him by the wrists; he looks at you like you are mad; your mother looks at you like you are mad.

"You didn't wash your hands," you say sternly.

You let him drop his arms. He breathes out and chuckles nervously. Even your mother laughs. Little does she realize you may have just saved her life.

Anyone who flies or has ever been in a hospital for a serious illness could have had similar experiences. The airplane tragedy did indeed happen to some poor souls who perished in a fatal 1935 airplane crash in Dayton, Ohio, in which the pilot forgot to release the elevator lock prior to takeoff. The standardized pilot's checklist that now defines aviation safety has its origin in that accident.

The pilot's checklist, refined over the years, has become the procedure followed in every cockpit on every commercial airline takeoff in America. It has become such a fundamental and effective part of preparation in the aviation industry that hospitals nationwide now hire pilots as consultants to help develop medical care checklists. Each year more than one million people contract staph infections in American hospitals, and more than one hundred thousand may die from them, according to the Association for Professionals in Infection Control and Epidemiology. The hospital checklist has become a key preparation tool in the national effort to reduce rampant staph and other infections and consequent deaths among patients.

Preparation is the basis for each checklist. Whether the task is flying a plane or administering a hospital, getting a road warrior home safely to that wonderful family or getting a vulnerable patient healthy again, preparation makes a vital difference between life and death.

Preparation, in less grave matters like business deals or contract negotiations or managing a staff or making family decisions, also makes the difference between success and failure. And the guarantor of proper preparation, even in more mundane matters, is the use of a preparation checklist.

For example, you are sitting in your office at nine in the morning and get a call from an important customer. She tells you that she could place a significant order for your newest product or service if you can agree upon the terms and have the deal "wrapped up by noon."

You ask some questions and determine that noon is a real

deadline. You ask about her alternatives to your product, as well as the customer's pricing goals.

She again says: "This has got to be done by noon."

You feel the pressure of wanting to do the deal. Your mind is racing a mile a minute about the pricing and delivery terms you want to propose to the customer. You want to get it done, but sense the danger of rushing.

What do you do now? This kind of challenge could arise with a client, family member, friend, or associate: deadlines *and* demands find their way into every relationship.

So the question may better be phrased as, Do you *dare to prepare?*

You do not have a lot of time. But almost any amount of time is sufficient to switch from reacting to preparing. Preparation means being proactive. So the best answer to the question of what you should do next is: ask the customer, "Can I call you back at 10:30?"

She likely will grant your request and you will have bought yourself some time to prepare methodically rather than merely react to her request. More important, if you work with the preparation principles that I overview in this introduction, you should be able to get a firmer grasp of the challenge you face. You should also be able to develop a presentation that is not doomed by a failure to analyze your objectives and develop a suitable strategy. Even ninety minutes of preparation will get you better results than just jumping in and responding to the customer's request. Preparation allows you to act instead of react.

Taking the time to prepare will help you achieve better results. Preparing methodically, even in a tight time frame, will help even more. Throughout my career I've had the

privilege of getting to know people from all walks of professional life—athletes, executives, entrepreneurs, musicians,
physicians, politicians—who are "master preparers." I profile them throughout the book, providing both exemplars and
methods to help you to respond to your own dare to prepare.

Preparation can be tough to define. In another context
involving a famous Supreme Court case, Justice Potter
Stewart had similar difficulty defining the word that was
central to the issue he and his fellow justices were faced
with: pornography. His definition was more intuitive than
legalistic: you certainly know it when you see it.

You might feel the same way about defining preparation.
So it could help a bit to think back to your grammar
school teachers who probably taught you that the best way
to define a word is to go back to the Latin. *Pre-* means
"before." *Pare*, according to *Cassell's Latin Dictionary*, can
mean "to supply or furnish." So, in essence, *prepare* means
to make it before you give it. You set up everything—you get
your ducks in a row—before you execute your task, sale,
throw, shot, incision, or legal argument. You make your
pitch or your case in your head. You visualize it. You assemble its parts. You piece it together before you do it, show it,
or speak it.

Methodical preparation is a part of American lore: Benjamin Franklin's pithy advice ("By failing to prepare, you are
preparing to fail"); Washington's preparation of a ragtag
colonial army to fight the world's greatest military power; the
planning that went into the D-day assault; the preparation at
NASA to meet Kennedy's charge to put a man on the moon.
We've all grown up hearing stories of heroic preparation.

I recently read Doris Kearns Goodwin's book about Abraham Lincoln, *Team of Rivals*. Frequent passages such as the following emphasize the importance to Lincoln of methodical preparation:

> Before speaking against the Nebraska Act, Lincoln spent many hours in the State Library, studying present and past Congressional Debates so that he could reach back into the stream of American history and tell a clear, reasoned, and compelling tale. He would express no opinion on anything, Herndon [Lincoln's law partner] observed, until he knew his subject "inside and outside, upside and downside."

My history professor at Haverford College, Roger Lane, looks to the first Europeans to arrive here for insight into a definition of preparation.

"The founding settlers, mainly Calvinists, believed that preparation in the world of business was important in earning God's favor toward you," Professor Lane said to me. "You had to earn it, and you earned it by preparing. There was a real theological dimension to the Protestant utilitarian work ethic. The religious aspect slowly faded, but even Ben Franklin's Poor Richard maxims were really the puritan ethic with the Calvinist theology drained out of it. There was a second wave of this preparation ethic with the Western European and Jewish immigrations, but those were really self-selecting groups of people who came here prepared with a purpose like the founding settlers did."

A complete definition of preparation for me is based on eight principles of preparation that I have developed after

nearly forty years as a businessman, attorney, and strategic
consultant. I follow these principles for the important business and personal undertakings in my life and use them as
well when I guide others. While the principles don't have to
be followed in rigid lockstep, there is a sequential logic to
them. They take the form of a checklist in the appendix
to this book. Their biggest benefit, I've found over the years,
is that they simply give you a greater sense of control and
competence. In brief they are:

1. **Understanding Your Objectives** is defining your
   endgame. What—simply and clearly—do you want to
   accomplish? How often have you said to yourself "I've got
   to get this done" without first defining what the endgame
   should be? All too often I see people put the cart before
   the horse. It is important to think clearly through what
   you want to accomplish rather than just following your
   gut. The long view and clear vision that come with well-
   defined objectives give you calmness and clarity.

2. **Planning with Precedents** provides examples of
   time-tested solutions to guide you and to help persuade other parties. Prior transactions, your experiences,
   or examples of others can influence your outcome or
   serve as a model. Precedents are found through reading,
   recording notes on previous experiences, discussing a
   task with a colleague or partner, or mulling through your
   mental catalogue of comparables.

3. **Knowing Your Alternatives** means laying out the
   various results you might attain, as well as the outcomes

your client or counterpart might expect. You make certain you are forecasting what you might be getting into.

4. **Defining the Interests** of the other party gets you focused on knowing the objectives or motives of the other side. You look beyond their stated positions. What needs do they have that you might be able to address?

5. **In Setting Your Strategy,** you establish a plan of action after analyzing the information you have gathered from the first four principles. With this information in hand, you determine the steps you will take and what you will ask of or say to your counterpart. With this principle, you also determine the manner, format, or tone with which you will convey your ideas or requests.

6. **Doing a Timeline** is synonymous with drudgery for some people. But a timeline is nothing more than an outline of projected dates aligned with key milestones. Timelines aren't taskmasters; they are tools to organize and lay out in front of you the steps that form your strategy.

7. **Picking Your Team** focuses on whom you will work with and what their roles and responsibilities will be. The key is matching people with their talents and interests. In addition, you look for a good devil's advocate.

8. **Writing Your Script** is jotting down the message or proposal you want to make as well as preparing the technique you will use to make it. By sketching the presentation of your message or proposal, practicing it, and sharing it with a team member, you check its effectiveness and gain confidence.

I have had the good fortune in my career to witness the preparation habits of people from all types of fields. Early on I served as Securities Commissioner for the State of Maryland. I founded a law firm and a publishing company. I became an accidental sports agent and built a sports management firm that has represented more Major League Baseball Hall of Famers than any other. And all of these endeavors led to my cofounding the Shapiro Negotiations Institute.

From these experiences it has become my personal conviction that cross-training—studying other fields for lessons—is as productive in business as it is in athletics. Advising surgeons, shortstops, violinists, and actors as well as CEOs and managers on preparation and negotiation has made me a better preparer in my other fields of work.

Whether you are a physician or an engineer, a real estate developer or a small business owner, a fund manager or a salesperson, a designer or a teacher, or engage in any professional endeavor or personal vocation, you will benefit from seeing how people from different, and perhaps unique, disciplines set their ducks in a row. Cross-training—analyzing the preparation of a leading investor, a world-class psychiatrist, a firefighter, a hostage negotiator, a college president, or a Major League Baseball general manager—will make you a better preparer and a more successful professional in your own line of work.

The people profiled in this book are primarily friends, colleagues, clients, and, in three cases, family. I picked them for their craftsmanship as preparers and also for their accessibility as symbols. They inspire others to prepare better. And they demonstrate that methodical preparation not only yields confidence and effectiveness, but also generates a satisfaction that works its way from professional activities into personal endeavors and interactions. They are, in alphabetical order:

R. W. Apple Jr. An associate editor, chief of several bureaus including Saigon, London, and Washington, D.C., and politics, travel, and food writer for the *New York Times*.

Ambassador Charlene Barshefsky. U.S. trade representative from 1996 to 2001, and senior international partner at WilmerHale LLP, Washington, D.C.

Steve Battista. The vice president of marketing for Under Armour performance apparel.

Steve Bisciotti. Founder of the Allegis Group, owner of the Baltimore Ravens, and member of the Forbes 400 list.

Taylor Branch. Pulitzer Prize–winning historian and author of the bestselling trilogy *America in the King Years*.

Gerald Brooks. A Baltimore County police detective and a member of its hostage negotiation team.

Dr. Benjamin Carson. Director of pediatric neurosurgery at Johns Hopkins Hospital and bestselling author.

Don Cohan. President of The Donesco Company, a real estate development firm, Olympic medalist in sailing, and cancer survivor.

Bob Costas. Emmy award–winning broadcaster and author of the bestselling book *Fair Ball: A Fan's Case for Baseball*.

J. Raymond DePaulo, Jr., MD. Henry Phipps professor and director. Psychiatrist-in-chief at Johns Hopkins Hospital.

John Dionne. Senior managing director of the Blackstone Group.

Joe Ehrmann. A minister, coach, and former NFL player who was named "The Most Important Coach in America" by *Parade* magazine.

Leon Fleisher. Concert pianist, teacher, and conductor.

Lisa Fontenelli. A managing director at Goldman Sachs and the chief operating officer of the Global Investment Research division.

Shirley Franklin. Mayor of Atlanta, Georgia, and formerly city manager for nine years.

Tom Giannopoulos. Chairman, president, and chief executive officer of MICROS Systems, Inc.

Larry Gibson. A law professor and campaign adviser for Liberian president Ellen Johnson Sirleaf, Madagascar president Marc Ravalomanana, and numerous American political leaders.

Liane Hansen. Host of National Public Radio's Weekend Edition Sunday.

Dr. Shari Huene-Johnson. Coordinator of leadership development for the Collier school district in Florida and former principal of the William S. Baer school.

Arnie Kleiner. President and general manager of KABC-TV in Los Angeles.

Andrew Klemmer. Founder and chief executive officer of the Paratus Group, an international project director for new museum construction.

Eric Mangini. Head coach of the New York Jets.

Joe Mauer. Catcher for the Minnesota Twins and American League batting champion in 2006.

Bill Miller. Chairman and chief investment officer of Legg Mason Capital Management.

Steve Mosko. President of Sony Pictures Television.

Robert Parker. Editor of *The Wine Advocate* and recipient of France's Chevalier de l'Ordre de la Légion d'honneur and named Commendatore in Italy's National Order of Merit.

Scott Pilarz, S.J. Jesuit priest, president of the University of Scranton, and professor of English literature.

Sam Presti. General manager of the Seattle Supersonics and former assistant general manager of the San Antonio Spurs.

Willie Randolph. Manager of the New York Mets, former New York Yankee's base and bench coach, and former Major League Baseball player.

Paul Sandler. Trial lawyer and partner at Shapiro Sher Guinot and Sandler, P.A.

Mark Shapiro. Executive vice president and general manager of the Cleveland Indians and Major League Executive of the Year in 2005.

Mayo Shattuck. Chairman and chief executive officer of the Constellation Energy Group.

Michelle Shepherd. Executive of the East Division of the Bank of America.

Ken Singleton. Broadcaster for the New York Yankees and former Major League Baseball player.

Dr. Henry Taylor. Senior associate in health policy and management for the Johns Hopkins Bloomberg School of Public Health and former West Virginia State health officer.

Ann Marie Tierney. A wildfire firefighter for Firestorm Wildland Fire Suppression in Chico, California.

Bill Walton. Chairman and chief executive officer of Allied Capital Corporation.

Wendy Webster. Store manager for Wegmans Food Markets, Inc.

Part 1

READY . . . SET . . .

1

PUT ME IN, COACH

You know the feeling—you first got it as a kid. Say you are a young musician taking lessons. You listen to your teacher play the piece for next week; you practice the most difficult chords with her; and you go home and nail it like Wynton Marsalis or Yo-Yo Ma. You tell yourself you've mastered it and decide to watch a sitcom instead of practicing more. You show up at your teacher's house seven days later, stretch your fingers, and utterly flub the recital.

Or say you're on the bench in youth basketball or in the Little League dugout, and you want to play. You can nail that shot; you can hit that pitcher. Coach turns to you; you get your chance; you rush in; and you miss the basket altogether or strike out on three pitches.

Most of you remember experiences like this as a kid. Comical or trite, they stick with you. And they serve as good analogies for trying to close a multimillion-dollar deal or sale, give a big presentation, do a negotiation, interview for a job, or pick a doctor. The exclamation "Put me in, Coach" didn't become a piece of Americana for nothing. It is the American way, in fact, to see or hear something done once and believe you can do it better. Immediately!

Whenever I hear John Fogerty's 1985 song "Centerfield," I laugh at the way I still feel the eagerness of a kid in the dugout when it comes to taking on a task. So hummable, the song captures the youthful zeal we can still feel when a big task is at hand. "Centerfield" became a favorite of my client and friend, the late Kirby Puckett, during the joyous ascent of the Minnesota Twins in the mid-1980s. Kirby had that Little League enthusiasm, and he made you feel as a fan that you could do it, too.

But let me tell you something: Kirby Puckett *practiced*, sportsese for "prepared," like his life depended on it. He was right up there with Cal Ripken Jr. in terms of a certain paranoia: I doubt either ever said "put me in, Coach" without feeling completely assured that he had prepared for all the possible dimensions of the at bat or of fielding the ball. Each man tempered his boyish zeal for the game with a studious devotion to preparation. On the scale of perspiration and inspiration, Cal and Kirby spent 50 percent of their time preparing and 50 percent performing. They perspired methodically during hours of practice and inspired monumentally when we were allowed to glimpse them perform.

For many reasons, the lionization of the master preparer seems to have waned. Performers are admired for their results, but not necessarily studied and emulated for their preparation. Enron was obviously a product of this do-it-quick culture. We live in what is perhaps the most results-driven era in history. Earnings, whether real or imagined, and performance, whether real or inflated, do not necessarily result from thorough preparation anymore. But, as a moralist at heart, I still believe that enduring success results from effective preparation. You can try to sneak around preparation, develop shortcuts, or come up with clever schemes. But succumbing to a shortcut culture will usually catch up with you.

THE GOOD OLD DAYS: WHEN YOUR MOTHER OR FATHER PREPARED LIKE THERE WAS NO TOMORROW

Doting elders of my family told me that I was going to be president of the United States. Most of you probably got that treatment, too. I was president of my high school and college classes. I began to believe the incessant familial hype and couldn't wait to turn thirty-five to qualify. Put me in, Coach, I can be president.

Your head is filled with images of winners. Particularly during the technology boom of the late 1990s and the real estate boom of this decade, people were becoming multimillionaires like never before. Understandably, a lot of people want to skip steps and rush into fame and fortune.

It took a wise man to slow me down. Soon after law

school, my uncles and aunts started asking me for tax advice, and I would give them answers based upon what I had learned in my studies. But as a lawyer for whom I worked, Robby Goldman, said to me: "Don't give advice unless it is based on your knowledge and experience." Robby forced me to learn to think and know before I spoke. He essentially was saying that even his own instruction was insufficient unless I practiced it myself.

Preparation mentors never stop coming into your life; when I started the Shapiro Negotiations Institute, I was in my fifties. Mark Jankowski, my partner, was in his thirties. I recognized Mark's skills and generational advantages and looked to him as a mentor. He taught me how technology could help a business become more productive and organized. We tend to think of mentors as our elders, and this is usually the case. But I realized you could open yourself up to mentors of any age; their experience, and your lack of it, should be the determining factor.

The greatest preparation mentor I ever had was my father. He was an immigrant from Russia with a primary school education and winning business skills. He owned a plumbing supplies company. When I grew old enough to work for him, I expected I would fill in alongside him in the office with my fancy brain and new calculator. But he put me in the warehouse to help manage the inventory and delivery of pipes and fittings. I loaded and unloaded trucks in the summer heat.

He said to me: "To do this business right you have to understand the underbelly of it."

I resented it, just as many of you no doubt resented your father or your first boss making you pay your dues. I resented it for a long time.

And then one day I understood. He kept me from rushing into the game; he forced me to prepare.

The apprenticeship process seems to be fading. This is emblematic of a broader departure from preparation, as you are pressed to multitask and produce more work product. You feel forced to find shortcuts for doing things. We all want to get into the game sooner. Of course, people still wink at preparation and work ethic, but a wink or a nod isn't what my father and his preparation generation had in mind. Along the way, we're losing some of the satisfaction and thoroughness that came with good, old-fashioned preparation.

Like some of you, I was lucky to grow up a son of the preparation generation. The preparation ethic was easier to instill because there simply were fewer distractions or excuses available to avoid it. My dad taught me to ignore the impulse and pressure to say "put me in, Coach." In essence, his message was: don't curb your enthusiasm, but harness it with a method. And don't make excuses about why you can't.

THE THREE EXCUSES, OR, WHY WE SAY WE DON'T NEED TO PREPARE

There are three common excuses for not preparing methodically and thoroughly:

1. I don't have time.

2. I've done this before.

3. I know how to do this.

"I DON'T HAVE TIME!":
THE GOTTA GET IT DONE TRAP

You probably remember a high school teacher or college professor's admonishment: you actually save time at the back end of a paper or project by preparing more thoroughly at the front end.

After a few frustrating efforts, you probably realized they were right: you actually have a less frustrating experience and superior result by slowing down at the beginning in order to thoroughly outline that term paper or presentation.

It's good advice that everyone knows makes sense. Why don't we follow it? The answer, I think, has a lot to do with technology that pushes you to multitask and engage in our speed-dial way of life. You have tools for instant access and instant response. You are told you can do more in less time and several things at once, so you do. It is incredible how busy you feel, and how little of substance you sometimes feel you actually produce.

In fact, I think I remember from high school physics that the key difference between speed and velocity is direction. Speed can take you in any direction, including round and round in a circle; velocity has a fixed direction. A preparation method transforms your excess speed into velocity. It harnesses your energy into direction.

Multitaskers are speedy. You're working your BlackBerry, cell phone, and computer; you're reading the stock market results; you're glancing at the newspaper—all at once. I actually used to read the newspaper at ball games or in the morning while I drove the car. So in my case, multitasking was not only a threat to the quality of my work, but to my clean driving record and health!

Once upon a time, e-mail was supposed to allow you to respond to some people on your own time. You could wait to respond to the e-mails until you were ready and had reflected on their queries or issues. Then along came the BlackBerry. E-mails acquired the urgency of phone calls.

Even recently I would leave the BlackBerry in vibration mode when I was in a meeting or even giving a speech. And nine times out of ten I would know who was calling and switch with the multitasker's second mind to think about the issue facing the caller while speaking to a dozen people in a conference room!

I still have concentration issues, and I've struggled with them since I was a young, up-and-coming multitasker. There was a television in my room and I would do my homework with it on. I had a little trick—a string on the off switch that I would pull when I heard my father's footsteps coming down the hall. I was already multitasking because of the intrusion of technology into my life.

Multitasking can result from technology or from peer pressure or from sheer hyperactivity. But you've got to shut it down and restore the methodical steps of preparation to turn speed into velocity. A preparation checklist (like the Preparation Principles Checklist in the appendix of this book) will help you do this and probably reduce your blood pressure along the way.

The heartening fact is that you will not only make fewer mistakes, but you will also enjoy what you do more. You will feel less rushed; you will feel like you have more time. And you will be able to say with confidence instead of arrogance: put me in, Coach!

The Two Powers of Nice—How Can That Be?

A recent coincidence reinforced my belief in the importance of methodical preparation. My first book, *The Power of Nice*, was about negotiations and was translated into four languages. My consulting firm, the Shapiro Negotiations Institute, trademarked the title of the book and still uses it as the program title in some of our courses. The title became a fundamental part of our brand and was closely associated with our consulting.

So I was surprised one day in the early summer of 2006 to receive a call from a friend who had read in *Newsweek* magazine about another forthcoming book entitled *The Power of Nice*. How could this be, I wondered? Was someone blatantly exploiting our trademarked phrase? Was it an effort to appropriate our brand?

I read the article and learned that the authors were the executives of Kaplan Thaler Limited, the advertising group in New York City. They were probably best known as the creators of the winning Aflac duck advertisements in which the woeful duck is always getting abused.

Although the article pointed to their *Power of Nice* as more of a life advice book (so not competitive with mine in terms of content), this was still an important issue for me and my firm. But, as usual, I was busy—about to leave with my wife on a vacation in Oregon. Adding to the time pressure was the fact that my partner Mark Jankowski was caring for his wife who had experienced a devastating illness.

I just didn't have the time to dig into the matter and knew what I wanted to do right away. I told myself: I don't have time to deal with this!

So I contacted the authors to ask them to consider using a different title that would not confuse readers with my book and my company's trademarked product. When I made the call, I hadn't fully prepared my strategy or scripted the conversation. The response from the person I spoke with was not good, and I was treated in a way that made me feel a wee bit like the abused and underappreciated Aflac duck.

During the call I was sitting in my office looking down at Baltimore's harbor. Water encourages reflection, and I realized—and not for the first time—that I had failed to practice what I preach.

By not sitting down with my team and thoroughly assessing the situation with a preparation method, I failed to methodically define my objectives, understand the other party's interests, forecast potential outcomes, and write a script to prepare for my encounter.

Now, I had plenty of good excuses to have rushed things. But no excuse is good enough to account for not preparing. Fortunately, it is never too late to prepare. Mark helped me recognize my error, and I rededicated myself and my team to preparing methodically. We analyzed the matter with the preparation checklist.

Methodical preparation transformed us from ugly ducks into well-prepared negotiators. We requested a copy of the authors' book in draft form and confirmed that the substance of each book was very different. We determined that the authors did not plagiarize our writing and ideas, but used a title without researching its prior use. And we realized we could propose a settlement that would avoid litigious nonsense and instead bring us a bit of a win from their book. Mark helped me to look at the issue succinctly when he said in an e-mail: "In order to continue to expand the brand of *The Power of Nice*, we will try to leverage a settlement agreement with these authors into an even higher profile for our book and concept."

By heeding my own advice and preparing methodically, we got the result we wanted. Kaplan Thaler agreed to acknowledge us and our trademark on its book's website with a link to our negotiations site; the authors mentioned the distinction between the two books in their book, and they provided other disclaimers. All of these concessions turned into additional marketing for a book that we published eight years ago. By scrutinizing our objectives, we prepared a proposal that made more sense than fighting over four simple words. By abandoning the excuse of having no time to prepare, I was able to aid our cause more effectively.

"I'VE DONE THIS BEFORE": THE REPETITION TRAP

The second excuse many people use for rushing the preparation process (or not preparing at all) is based on the results of past experience. You are giving the same speech to a new audience, making the same product presentation to a new customer, or negotiating a real estate contract for the thousandth time. You know your way around this situation like the high school history teacher who is teaching the

American Revolution for the tenth straight year. But no matter how good you have gotten at the routine, there is almost always one new nuance that differentiates the new performance for your audience.

That was the case when I taught law. We used the case method year in and year out. I was busy with other jobs, so I sometimes shortcut my preparation because I had taught the course the previous year. I said to myself: "I've done this before." So rather than dig in and realize how my professional experience may have changed my interpretation of the case, I coasted. And rather than enrich my mind and my instruction with insights from new students, I stuck with my course notes from past years. I could have taken the class to a whole new level of scholarship and instruction. I still regret that and vowed years ago to never make the same mistake.

On a more mundane level, here's another example. I'd say I use a chain saw on our farm once a year after a big storm blows through. Because I've successfully used it before, I am always initially inclined to lock and load—an approach fraught with danger. But thank goodness for my wife and her reliable warnings. One look at her and instead of just forgetting all the safety issues, I reread the instruction manual and safety tips each time.

Indeed, the Centers for Disease Control and Prevention reports that each year approximately thirty-six thousand people are treated in emergency rooms for injuries using chain saws! How many of them said: "I've done this before"?

Or think back to the introduction to this book: that veteran pilot in the front of your plane looking at the black book and thoroughly reviewing the pilot's checklist. You get the sense—and the assurance—that he or she is treating your flight as his or her first flight despite having made thousands of them.

The habit of methodical preparation can grow into a default system for personal or professional endeavors. The Preparation Principles Checklist in the appendix helps me resist the knee-jerk excuse of saying "I've done this before."

The Failed Courtship of a Great Slugger and Hometown Boy

The wisdom gained from hard experience has taught me not to say, "I've done this before." Indeed, one of the toughest lessons for me was the time I lost the opportunity for my sports firm to represent the great slugger Mark Teixeira.

Baseball's abiding sentimentality makes a hometown star one of the delights of the game. The occurrence is rare: Cal Ripken Jr., who grew up near Baltimore; Joe Mauer, a Minnesota boy; the return of Roger Clemens, a legend from his days at the University of Texas, to play for the Houston Astros. So when Mark was slugging his way through high school baseball in my hometown of Baltimore, I felt very confident that my sports firm would end up representing him.

Mark was known to be a big Orioles fan; he came from a strong and famously grounded family; and we had even met on one occasion. What's more, his baseball coach was a friend of a former client, the Hall of Famer and Orioles third baseman Brooks Robinson.

Even a key business associate told me that he thought that a relationship with Mark was likely as he approached his decision to select an agent and turn professional.

So, subconsciously, I did not prepare for my meeting with Mark and his family as methodically or even as vigorously as I usually do. I said to myself, everyone is telling me this is destiny. A local kid and a good family meet a local sports firm known for a high standard of values and relationships in a morally problematic business. I said to myself, I've done this before.

What had I done before? At my sports firm, we target clients just like Mark. We have represented Brooks, Cal Jr., Kirby Puckett, and later Joe Mauer. We are small and want to stay small, and we strive to find clients who want life coaches as much as contract negotiators.

So I generally prepare for meeting this sort of client and his parents by proceeding through my preparation principles. In particular, I focus on four of the principles: objectives, precedents, alternatives, and interests. I set our objectives of making clear our desire to engage in a long-term relationship, collaborate with the client in building a solid personal brand, and earn a competitive fee. I look thoroughly at precedents—the scripts and notes from previous presentations. And I prepare to cite some of these precedents in the meetings with the potential client. I look at alternative ways to structure the potential client's goals prior to the Major League Baseball draft and discuss this at the presentation. And I try to determine clearly the interests of the client: How important is money to him? What kind of organization would fit his personality? How important are family and friends and relationships in general? What other agents is he considering?

I did very little of this as we prepared to present our firm to Mark Teixeira. I said, I've done this before, and my track record speaks for itself. Guess who got to represent Mark? Scott Boras. Yes, the guy who got Alex Rodriguez the contract the size of the GDP of some small nations. The guy loved by players seeking fortunes and feared by ownership and management for his winning track record.

Scott came onto my turf and beat me at my own game. I no longer was confidently saying, I've done this before. I was struggling to answer to myself as I asked over and over, What have I done?

In fact, my partner and I were trying to downsize the business. Tired of unrealistic parents of athletes, we decided to handpick our clients based on a whole set of increasingly unconventional, old-school criteria like intelligence, integrity, and simply enjoyment. But Mark fit these criteria perfectly, and so did his family. I blew it. I walked into the meeting coasting on my career and my reputation as a good guy in Baltimore. I did not have a deep understanding of the family's financial objectives or Mark's professional and educational goals. I did not probe them with questions about what they looked for in an organization. I did not present a thorough negotiating plan. I did not prepare methodically.

Mark has gone on to become one of the best players in baseball. I have enjoyed watching him play, especially when his team comes to Baltimore. He embodies professionalism and preparation. And whenever I see Mark walk to the plate, I remember the lesson from my poor preparation. The haunting question "What have I done?" is so painful that I don't ever again want to use the excuse "I've done this before."

"I KNOW HOW TO DO THIS": THE SUCCESS SYNDROME

You see the task at hand, albeit a new one. You are the kind of person who tends to be successful at whatever you do. And, full of confidence, you say to yourself: "I know how to do this." And with this certainty, you decide that you can shortcut the preparation needed to perform the task well.

How many times have you walked into a room that looks a bit drab? The walls are scarred and dented. You go to the paint store, select a nice color, and buy the brushes and pans and rollers. You have not painted a room before, but you've seen it done and it looks so easy. You say to yourself, "I know how to do this."

You pour the paint into the pan, set up the ladder, and start rolling that rich blue paint onto the wall. You are so satisfied until your neighbor walks in and asks when you applied the primer. Primer?

Confidence can quickly spill over into arrogance. Saying "I know how to do this" can become a bad habit—whether you are painting a room or doing something for the first time in your professional life.

By using a methodical approach to preparation despite initial impulses to rush in, you prevent yourself from making errors of arrogance. The principles of preparation keep you humble and hungry. Preparation keeps your feet on the ground. It keeps you from sounding like the guy who always steps up and says, "I know how to do this."

The Education of One of the Best Broadcasters in the Business

Ken Singleton

Ken Singleton has been a baseball broadcaster for about twenty-five years, working for the fearsome George Steinbrenner since 1997. He is one of the most popular broadcasters in the history of one of the legendary sports franchises in the world. And Ken never even played for the Yankees! Indeed, as a longtime Baltimore Oriole, he had been a Yankee killer!

How did a folksy and gentlemanly ex–big leaguer become one of the most respected broadcasters in the business? How did Ken win the praise of even the legends Vin Scully and Jack Buck?

He resisted the temptation to say, "I know how to do this." As a player, Ken gave thousands of interviews in front of the camera. He combined charisma and intelligence in a way few athletes do. He could easily have done what a lot of former stars do: ride the coattails of celebrity right into the broadcast booth and last a couple of years before their audience grows tired of their hollow insights and gimmicky commentary. Even before he ended his playing career, Ken knew that to succeed in his next career he could not afford to say, "I know how to do this."

In 1980, Ken and I sat down and plotted out his objectives and strategy for succeeding as a broadcaster. We looked at the precedents of ex-players who had both succeeded and failed, and we determined that Ken should learn broadcasting from the inside out.

We accessed our good relationships with local television executives to develop internships with local channels during the off-season. Ken learned to edit, to "cut tape" as they say in the business, to construct a piece, and to ask tight questions. He learned his way around the byzantine offices of television stations. He learned the importance of camaraderie and teamwork among a sports news team and between announcers and producers and fixers and drivers.

Then, during the awful Major League Baseball strike of 1981, Ken actually got a job with Channel 11 in Baltimore and did his own stories with a full production crew showing him the ropes. He worked as a sportscaster while he waited to resume his baseball career.

"Those internships and learning the business on the inside made all the difference in my career," Ken said. "It is true that a lot of big leaguers think they can walk right into the booth. To make it at the level of professional baseball, you have to be brimming with confidence anyway. But it would have been a huge mistake to apply that to something off the field."

Ken spent over ten years announcing games for the Expos and Blue Jays in Canada and then landed an interview with his old nemesis on the ballfield, the dreaded Yankees.

"I will never forget walking into Mr. Steinbrenner's office at Legends Field in Tampa," Ken said. "He didn't stand up to shake my hand and I thought I was already in trouble. Then he said 'It's hard for me to feel okay about someone doing this who was not a Yankee.' I told him I was just doing my job as an Oriole and that at least I grew up in New York. He said, 'Our fans aren't going to like you because of all the

bad things you used to do to us.' Then we kept talking and
he referred to a producer and said, 'You'll like him when
you meet him.' I went home and told my wife I thought I
had a shot."

The next day Ken got the job, and he has one of the
longest tenures of any announcer in baseball. He resisted
the arrogant athlete's impulse to say, "I know how to do
this." He prepared methodically to be a broadcaster. I bet
Steinbrenner and the managers at the Yankees' YES Network sensed this years ago when they hired Ken.

2

"I WOULD LIKE TO THANK THE LORD JESUS CHRIST AND ERIC MANGINI"

So put yourself in this scenario: you love your daughter as much as humanly possible. She meets a fine young man, but you want to study him for a while to be certain he is perfect for her. A year later, you find what might be a flaw. But the flaw is actually a good one, a sign of character and conviction: he works too hard. He can relax and loves being with family. But he is utterly driven—not so much by success as by doing things right no matter how long it takes.

This was my predicament when my daughter Julie fell in

love many years ago with Eric Mangini, the current head coach of the New York Jets and one of the youngest head coaches in National Football League history. I have rarely met many people who work as much as Eric. Nor have I ever met someone who prepares so methodically for his work. Using a preparation system, Eric and his staff transformed a struggling team into a contender during the 2006 season.

Being a head coach in the NFL is a grueling and all-consuming job. Professional football is a business in which the world's most talented players and coaches function under the newfangled sports socialism of a salary cap and profit sharing. The result is a unique parity throughout the league. So one of the decisive factors in winning is preparing better than other teams. Most teams are preparing all the time: grueling practices year-round, endless sessions watching game film, scouting departments full of hungry young people dying to make their living in the sport. So preparing better cannot mean preparing more. In the NFL, it means preparing more methodically—having the superior system of preparation.

Even if you are not a football fan, Eric's approach will help you understand how using a system like the preparation principles to structure your preparation will help you increase the chances of success in both your professional and personal lives.

This became apparent to me after the American Football Conference Championship game in 2004. Eric was then the secondary coach of the New England Patriots for head coach Bill Belichick. Their secondary that year had suffered innumerable injuries, and Eric was forced to remake offensive players like Troy Brown into defensive players.

Belichick is the quintessential method man, so Eric had a

good teacher. And when it came to patching together a presentable secondary, Eric focused on teaching and constantly rehearsing a cohesive defensive scheme rather than emphasizing man-to-man coverage and individual talents. His secondary seemingly thought and moved as one entity. Their awareness of one another's assignments and position on the field was uncanny. The system, and its preparation, helped the undermanned group become a startlingly effective one.

So after the victory in the AFC Championship, safety Rodney Harrison was so joyous during an interview on national television that he shouted: "I would like to thank the Lord Jesus Christ and Eric Mangini!"

Now, I cannot recall ever hearing a professional player thank an assistant coach. You hear Jesus thanked an awful lot, also Mom, and occasionally the head coach. But an assistant coach? My son-in-law? We replayed the moment, and I immediately realized that Rodney Harrison was essentially acknowledging the value of Eric's methodical preparation.

The players' praise continued through Eric's first year as head coach of the New York Jets.

Prior to the Jets' first playoff game under Eric in early 2007, Kimo von Oelhoffen, a grizzled veteran of the NFL and former member of the Super Bowl champion Pittsburgh Steelers, called Eric the best prepared coach he had ever seen.

"I've learned more football from that man in one year than I've learned in a long time," the thirteen-year veteran told the New York Post. "He doesn't leave one stone unturned. He will rep it and rep it until we can freakin' do it. He works harder than anybody I've ever seen. You trust people like that. He gets his point across and makes sure that everybody in the room knows his role, his responsibility, and the game plan. We go through every situation, and when those situations arise, we know how to respond. We don't make many mental mistakes."

The first time Eric and I talked about his system, we realized that his buzzwords—objectives, precedents, alternatives, scripting—could fall right into the preparation checklist that I teach.

"Our whole business is based on preparation," Eric said. "The whole week is designed to get the maximum level of preparation and therefore effectiveness. We have a sign on our practice field with a quote from the decathlete Dan O'Brien. It says 'The will to succeed is nothing without the will to prepare.' Everyone wants to be successful. At this level, everyone has enormous talent. We stress not just the preparation as a group but the importance of individual preparation. And it's not just when we are in the building. It's what you're doing when you're not in the building, too."

Eric makes a key point—preparation takes a strong will. He reminds me of a famous comment made by the baseball coach and manager Cal Ripken Sr.: "Perfect preparation makes perfect." The willingness to slow down, to apply a method, and to proceed step-by-step has a lot to do with being a great head coach or manager of any team of people.

Eric even prepares the Jets' training facility.

"Everything is geared toward progress in all areas," he said. "When we got here, the tables in the dining room were all circular. I had a friend from Australia visiting and he commented how in Australian military prep schools they believe long tables foster a sense of teamwork and unity. So we put in long tables. You don't know what will make the difference. We try to design everything to create the most effective environment for preparation."

The extremely competitive and imitative world of professional football won't allow Eric to reveal some of his more innovative preparation methods. But a look at one amazing game in his first year as head coach illuminates his use of many of the preparation principles.

Obviously, Eric's primary objective is to win. He makes that very clear. In the second week of November 2006, the Jets were preparing to play Eric's former team, the New England Patriots. The press had made much of the budding rivalry between Eric, the young protégé, and Belichick, his mentor. The Patriots had become a sports dynasty—remarkable for the development of players, their cohesion as a team, and their precision. They had become the New York Yankees of the 1990s or the Los Angeles Lakers of the 1980s.

Eric's tough and upstart squad had already lost to the Patriots once in 2006. In New York, no less. So in a sport where the home field advantage is very significant, the Jets would be traveling to Boston to try to stay in the hunt for a playoff bid against Eric's professional football alma mater.

So how did Eric prepare his team for such a daunting task?

First, he stayed focused more than ever on his two fundamental strategies: slowing down the game and improving communication. These two strategies are the foundation of the weekly scripting that Eric and his coaches do with the team. The weekly regimen—installing plays, walking through them, then going through them at half speed, then moving through them repeatedly at full speed, and then reviewing them on film—is designed to prepare the players to intuitively execute a script.

Eric emphasizes visualization and repetition to give the players the sensation that the whole field is moving more slowly during the real game.

"Michael Jordan always used to say that one of the reasons he prepared so hard is because when he does get into that moment it slows down for him," Eric said.

Second, Eric respects the daunting complexity of having eleven people move seamlessly as one entity, particularly in a stadium with eighty thousand screaming fans. His weekly preparation method is geared toward developing "aggressive communication." He picks his coaching staff in large part based on his analysis of their communication skills; he drafts players whom he thinks will be able to communicate clearly with coaches and teammates. Aggressive communication is a strategy that requires a coaching staff and team that likes to have things clear. Very clear.

"Communication is such a huge issue in football," Eric said. "Eleven people are making the same decision at the same time. We are always looking to create opportunities to increase the level of communication here. We even keep tape of unexpected or unusual game situations in our library to study. You are just preparing for every possible moment."

Eric looked to precedents like all this game tape to help him refine his strategy for this particularly challenging game. For example, he studied the Patriots' games in weather conditions like he knew they would encounter this November Sunday. He took advantage of an extra week off for the Jets to review yards and yards of video of the Patriots. He mined his own recollection of the Patriots' tendencies and strategies from his days as a coach there. And, with a little cooperation from Mother Nature, he added a very specific wrinkle to his communication strategy.

Jeffri Chadiha, a writer from *Sports Illustrated*, took notice of this strategic addition:

> Visitors to the Jets' training facility at Hofstra University on Nov. 8 might have been a bit puzzled by what they saw. In a driving rain, players and coaches splashed through their drills as loud music blared from speakers along the sidelines. For a few sessions the Jets even moved from the field turf to the muddy grass. All the while the team's warm, dry indoor practice field stood in the background, unused.

Eric had developed another strategy because of the precedents he had studied: to replicate playing conditions as closely as possible. In the rain and din of their practice field, the Jets were trying to implement their strategy—to slow down the game and communicate effectively—in conditions that undermined cohesion and communication. Eric knew that the field in New England famously turned to slop during the type of weather that was being forecast for the coming Sunday.

The result of the rain, mud, loud music, and slow motion that constituted Eric's methodical preparation: a 17–14 Jets upset! The field was absolute mud by the end. The uniforms of both teams were brown. Eric barely cracked a smile. The Jets' players looked like they were doing a rain dance together in celebration at midfield.

I remember one drenched and muddied player saying in

an interview on the field that the Jets won because they had already played the game during the week.

New England Pro Bowl defensive end Richard Seymour told the *Boston Herald*: "They outplayed us and outcoached us." To me, that translated into "outprepared us."

Herald writer Gerry Callahan wrote that Eric's team "would run through the walls for him, but only in the precise order and sequence that he taught them."

You sense Eric's insistence on precise order and sequence when you watch him lead a practice or interact with his staff. You sense it when he walks into a room. His preparation system is insistently methodical. When he first started as the Jets' head coach, that insistence consistently irritated some veterans. Some players complained about the rigidity and repetition. But games like the upset in the Boston mud changed all that. In fact, the Patriots even changed the surface of their field soon after the Jets' big game.

The Jets will win and lose games through the years because some teams may be more talented, some players may be injured, or some unlucky bounces may go against them. The vagaries of the NFL—losing a key player due to a contract dispute or having your quarterback get hurt in the first game of the season—can undermine the best-laid plans for success. But I doubt that they will ever lose for lack of preparation.

The Jets, like any team or company, cannot succeed on preparation alone. What economists like to refer to as "extrinsic events"—shocks to the supply chain or currency devalutions—have their football equivalent in quarterback controversies or injuries.

As most football fans know, 2007 was a rough season for

the Jets. Lots of so-called "extrinsic events," and even some internal miscalculations. But what has impressed me about Eric is his continued commitment to his preparation method in spite of the challenges thrown at his team. If anything, the struggles in 2007 reinforced the importance of his system for him more than the surprising success of 2006. No doubt Eric never took seriously his fleeting New York nickname, "Mangenius." He knows full well that preparers are rarely geniuses, but always perserverers who rely on a system through thick and thin.

When you spend time with Eric, he reminds you of an old-school craftsman. He could be a stonemason building a wall. His preparation is his craft. He takes pride in it as much as in winning. And he teaches his players to rely on and take satisfaction from a systematic approach to their jobs, too.

The lesson of Eric Mangini reminds me of something I say over and over again to my clients, colleagues, and seminar participants: the only thing you really control in life is your preparation. You may be up against more devious, more intelligent, or more excitable people, but you can't control their conduct, steal their skills, or tranquilize their emotions. You can't control external events. But if you prepare yourself and your team fully, you know that you will have done all you can do to achieve an optimal result. For me, the preparation principles, to which I now turn, are the best way to control the only thing you can control: your methodical preparation.

Part 2

THE PRINCIPLES

• Objectives • Precedents • Alternatives
• Interests • Strategy • Timeline
• Team • Script

3

WHAT'S YOUR DESTINATION?

Understand Your Objectives

Energy and motivation are wonderful to behold. But without a direction, they can have you spinning in circles and wondering why you aren't accomplishing what you set out to do. A three-word question helps you define your objectives and is the best way to begin any task. What and why? That is, what do you want to accomplish and why are you doing it? The answer to the question clarifies the reason you are undertaking a task and constitutes the first step in preparation.

Lest you think that taking the time to clearly define your objectives slows you down, my experience is that it is an essential step in pushing performance from acceptable to exceptional. You are one of thousands of talented and dedicated people in your field. Better performance and greater satisfaction require harnessing motivation with a clear understanding of your objectives. Definition is the differentiator.

Say you catch the fever to climb Mt. Everest, as has been the case with an increasing number of mountaineers. Implicit is the goal to make it to the top. But unless you clearly spell out the objective to include coming down safely, your ultimate strategy for a safe return may fail as it has for an increasing number of climbers.

Say you get a big promotion, and it is your assignment to fill your previous position. The two candidates are two of your closest friends in your company. Rather than offend either, you come up with a compromise that splits the job into two positions. Your boss approves it. A year later, you realize clarity and accountability demand a single person in one position. Your shared leadership plan results in their passing the buck to each other; they argue over who should make decisions; their staff gets confused. Intuition and impulsiveness caused you to make a decision without clearly understanding your objective of having accountability and responsibility in the position. Had you fully defined your objective, you would have found another way to preserve the friendships as well as the integrity of the position.

Intuition and its dangerous relative, impulsiveness, often convince you that it is okay to skip this preparation principle. It may often be the case that you undertake a task without fully defining your objectives; that is, you rush right in without pausing to understand why you are doing something and where you want it to take you or your project. And consequently, since the preparation principles are linked sequentially, you undermine the added value of each subsequent principle, and the preparation process falls short.

Defining your objectives is the first domino that tips over the others on the path toward proper preparation.

Can you imagine being told to slow down in business or in life to succeed? I still sometimes struggle to ignore those cultural voices telling us that we should follow our gut and trust our instinct. Preparation involves perpetual humility.

Call it purpose-driven work: the best work is done with a clearheaded understanding of its purpose. Don't do it just because your boss said to do it. Don't do it just because your gut tells you it is the thing to do.

In 1986, baseball was struggling with a drug crisis. I discussed the problem regularly with some of my clients. Our gut told us to reach out to the fans through the press and tell them my clients were clean. Instead, we slowed down and used clearly defined objectives to build a program that might have served the game as an example over twenty years later.

COMING CLEAN ABOUT DRUGS

Today's baseball fans have lived in trying times. The steroid plague and the failure to implement an effective testing policy gave the game a reputation of shadows and slipperiness. What was real and what was chemical? Who was telling the truth and who was fibbing? What hits come from talent and preparation and what home runs come from injections?

Baseball fans may also recall a drug plague in the early and mid-1980s. Then the drug was cocaine, an outgrowth, some said, of rampant amphetamine use in the game. Drug busts of players on the Kansas City Royals and the Pittsburgh Pirates, among others, alarmed fans to the point of revolt. The game was jeopardizing its kid-friendly reputation, and fans were irate.

In 1986, I represented many of the players on the major-league roster of the Baltimore Orioles. Most of them were very solid citizens who cared deeply about the integrity of their profession. They wanted to speak out against drugs but not betray teammates or the camaraderie of their fellow players.

Both of these objectives struck me as honorable, albeit sometimes contradictory. And so I sat down with groups of my players and probed their objectives and encouraged them to do the same. We collectively realized that this was a group that had really dedicated themselves to being citizens of their community. And the best way to demonstrate their values to their fans would not be through the press but through some sort of tangible proof.

So we developed this objective: "In order to demonstrate to our city that this problem is isolated and not affecting this team, we will develop and participate voluntarily in a drug-testing program for the entire season." All but a handful of players on the team and all of the management agreed to submit to a yearlong drug-testing program administered by Johns Hopkins School of Medicine. It would be rigid and scientific and random.

At the end of the year, the bond between the fans of Baltimore and the Orioles players was stronger than ever. A by-product was a statement made to the Players Association and Major League Baseball that the will for grassroots change among players existed. A clear understanding of objectives by a unique group of young men led to an exemplary result.

The point is that reflection hones intuition. Your initial impulse may point you in the right direction, but the key is to clarify, refine, or even re-define your objectives.

Next in this chapter I profile three people who understand their objectives: entrepreneur and Forbes 400 member Steve Bisciotti, Dr. Henry Taylor of Johns Hopkins School of Public Health, and banker Michelle Shepherd. As a businessman, Steve focuses on aligning his objectives with his specific talents better than anyone I have met. Henry slows down and clarifies his objectives despite the urgency and complexity of international health crises. And Michelle uses the clarity achieved with the repetition of objectives to help a large and disparate team work together toward a common goal.

ALIGNING YOUR OBJECTIVES WITH YOUR TALENTS

Steve Bisciotti

Steve Bisciotti, with his gruff voice and gregarious manner, strikes you more as a Pro Bowl football player than a young NFL owner. And when he starts to speak about his career, he has the eyes of a linebacker—darting, intense, and focused on the objectives.

Steve hones his objectives to fit his strengths. He has a keen self-awareness that helps him clearly define and stay dedicated to his targets. Nothing shows this more than the way Steve set his primary objective to build a great company based on his peerless sales abilities. Another objective—providing financial security for his family after losing his father at an early age—provided the motivation for fulfilling the first. Steve set his eyes on these two clear objectives and never blinked. You get the sense that he wakes up every morning and recounts each objective—one, two, three, four—before he begins his day.

Steve founded Allegis Group, a technical services and recruiting company, when he was twenty-three years old and had just $3,500 in the bank. He had been fired from his first job and was living with two friends who were bartenders in a town house in Annapolis, Maryland; Steve asked them if he could convert their basement into his headquarters. One of the bartenders became his first employee, his cousin became his partner and business manager, and Steve used his sales skills to grow a multibillion-dollar company in the course of a decade. Today he owns the NFL's Baltimore Ravens.

When he was eight years old, Steve lost his father to leukemia. You ask him to talk about his laserlike focus on objectives and this is the first thing he brings up.

"From the day my dad died, my mother was constantly talking to us about the real reason we were doing things, the real objective of any activity," Steve said. "It was like suddenly you realized the urgency of everything, the need to have a clear objective."

So Steve realized his first objective in life and business even before he was a teenager: to be able to leave his family on solid financial footing were he to die at age thirty-five like his father.

That is a pretty intense objective. I can relate to it because my father died when I was sixteen. I admired him the way Steve admired his father. Their early deaths, Steve says, "fix them in some sort of stasis—they are always admirable and always perfect in our image of them."

Our objectives can come from uncanny, almost biological sources. They can even come from tragedy.

Steve clearly links not only his professional and financial success, but also his value system, to the loss of his father and his mother's rallying of the family.

"My only objective in the early days was to be rich enough when I died at thirty-five that my wife and kids wouldn't have to work," Steve said. "It was that simple."

But Steve's mother helped him establish another critical objective that he exercises to this day: seek and value character over competence. Steve struggled in school. He had a hard time with memorization and fought to pay better attention in class.

"There were no redeeming qualities to education in my book," Steve said. "I don't like saying that now as a parent. But then I knew what I was good at and what my mother wanted me to be good at."

So when he would return home from school with poor grades, his mother would first confirm that he had put forth his best effort. And then she would evaluate him on things like his manners, character, and determination as if she were grading a homework assignment. And she would encourage him to be a salesman.

"She loved business accomplishment almost as much as she loved personal ethics and morality," Steve said. "So even though I failed at school she made me proud to achieve in things like good manners, character, and integrity. And she knew early on that I was going to be a salesman. She saw it in me and brought that talent out of me when I was struggling with more orthodox measures of talent like school."

So the professional objective—to be a great salesman—became a fundamental part of Steve's life as a teenager. The decision to sell services and not products came when he had to select a job from the three offers he got upon graduation from Salisbury State College.

"Selling Monroe computers, selling medical supplies, or working in the temp industry selling services," Steve said. "The guy who hired me changed my life. He said that if you take a job selling products you can always be outdone no matter how hard you work. Somebody may simply want the IBM instead of the Monroe. In the services industry you can't be outdone by a product. So my objective to become a great salesman became even clearer."

Steve was essentially a one-man band when he soon set off on his own to form Allegis. He was trying to outwork his competitors by phoning engineers from 7 A.M. to 10 P.M., covering both East and West Coast workdays when his East Coast competitors went home at 6 P.M. After hours and in between calls and trips, he did his own accounting, met with his attorney, and paid bills. He did it all well, but felt the back office business obligations distracted him from the objective of being the very best salesman he could be.

"I knew I was a born salesman—I instinctively knew how to make people want to give me business," Steve said. "But I was struggling to pull it all together. I was getting depressed. So I called a guy from my neighborhood who was a mentor to ask how to pull the business together."

Heeding the advice, Steve brought in his cousin, a CPA, as a major shareholder and rededicated himself exclusively to sales. And then Allegis really took off.

And that rapid success allowed Steve to realize another objective—being in the sports business—that he had always harbored but never allowed himself to focus on because of his commitment to the primary ones of supporting his family and being an unrivaled salesman. Steve had always loved sports, and for many years he dreamed of running a team.

So when the opportunity arose to purchase the Baltimore Ravens NFL franchise, Steve set a very specific, twofold objective. First, it was common knowledge that Art Modell, then the Ravens' owner, was struggling financially and essentially had to sell the team to leave his own family on solid financial footing. So Steve wanted the transaction to respect Art's legacy to the NFL. Second, Steve realized that this transaction would take him outside of the one business he knew he had mastered—sales. And he knew he had decided early on in his life to eliminate distractions and maintain his focus on his area of expertise. So he set an objective that became the premise for the transaction: he wanted to stage his purchase of the team in a way that allowed Art Modell to transition out of majority owner-ship and allowed Steve to transition into a new field of business.

With the help of some talented attorneys and accoun-tants, Steve and Art staged a four-year transition in owner-ship in which Steve would first become a minority owner and then eventually a majority owner and leave Art a very small share in the franchise.

"To do business the way my mother insisted I do business,

I had to honor Art in that way," Steve said. "At the same time I had a lot to learn and also had the objective of slowly making a positive impression on the community. The transition phase was self-serving in a way, but also the best combination for both Art and me. It was a win-win."

The structure was very innovative in the business of professional sports. Usually a wealthy purchaser of a franchise can't wait to take control and revel in the acclaim and excitement of professional sports. But Steve set the distinct objective of learning the business and supporting Art.

In the meantime, he also used the interregnum to evaluate the Ravens' business and coaching staff to determine whom he would retain or replace.

Disdainful of distraction, Steve devotes himself to ownership with the same singularity of purpose with which he worked the telephone for fifteen hours a day as a salesman in the basement of a bachelor's town house.

Steve Bisciotti woke up at age twenty-three and went to work like he might die at thirty-five. He kept his linebacker eyes on his objectives and realized them by the age his father was when he passed away. Steve kept his objectives to a handful, tailored them to his strengths, and pursued them relentlessly.

THE OBJECTIVE IS GLOBAL PREPARATION

Dr. Henry Taylor

If you have not died from avian flu by now, you might want to find a way to thank Dr. Henry Taylor and his colleagues at the Johns Hopkins Bloomberg School's Center for Public Health Preparedness.

The name of the center says it all—Preparedness.

The preparation objective at the Center is simple: control or even eliminate public health epidemics around the globe. Henry and his colleagues sharpen this objective by breaking it down into two components: the transformation of social structures so some struggling communities can better tend to their own health, and the analysis of the stages of disease and epidemics in order to precisely time research expenditures, political lobbying, and public intervention.

Henry illustrates how you set clear objectives by slowing down and cutting through the clutter and complexity of a challenge. His field is public health, but the manner in which he clarifies his objectives is applicable in any professional or business pursuit.

This Hopkins school, in whose growth Henry's father played an instrumental role, houses some of the most bustling, constant preparers you will ever meet. Imagine the trading floor of a stock exchange, but here the professors and students and community activists and government leaders are exchanging ideas about epidemics and disease. You hear numerous languages, see several shades of skin, and feel a satisfying "globalness" to which the United Nations can only aspire.

These constant preparers thrive on two paradoxes: success never comes, and results are achieved only when something doesn't happen.

Success never comes because bacteria and viruses are constantly evolving as a part of the global biological system of which we form a mere part.

And these preparers do not know when to celebrate—in fact, they never can completely celebrate a result—because there is no finite moment when they know that the disease or epidemic has been defeated or that a new one is not racing around the corner.

In public health, preparation of the many depends upon the mostly invisible preparation by the few, and some of those few are scurrying through the halls of the Center for Public Health Preparedness. Not aware of it, we are all in the hands of these health professionals dedicated to preparing us for the next epidemic. Our obliviousness is not so much a basic right as a product of the work and constant preparation of these public health professionals.

Henry carries a little bottle of alcohol-based hand disinfectant in his backpack; books with titles like *The Sources and Modes of Infection* and *The Swine Flu Affair* line the bookshelf of his spartan office; he analyzes the spread of germs at the cafeteria counter for you as you line up to pay for your lunch. The reality of the bacterial and viral world— the risks and complexities of microbes—would probably overwhelm most of us with anxiety. But for Henry it is a never-ending source of intellectual excitement and social commitment.

Having clear objectives is essential to succeeding in this high-stakes mission.

"The critical issue, perhaps for the future of the human race, is grassroots community engagement in general and the empowerment of women in health care worldwide in particular," Henry said. "Networking among women in terms of health is the key to wholesale change in health care and lifestyle. It is a fact that women and particularly mothers are the ones who drive and achieve lifestyle change. We are at the very early stages of instituting this change, but it is catching fire. By 2020 the community networking will be extensive."

What can tempt public health professionals away from this networking objective? Henry believes it is the disease-of-the-month club mentality driven by politicians and celebrities, as well as a fixation with pharmaceuticals.

"Our approach is contaminated by the notion of magic bullets," Dr. Taylor noted. "Take MRSA, or methicillin resistant staph infections. Interaction between humans and infections goes back to the beginning of time. But now, because we have overprescribed antibiotics for things like the flu for which they do not work, the bacteria have adapted and are defeating the pharmaceutical process."

Like many of his colleagues, Henry is committed to the objective of seeking a more community-based approach that puts prevention first and uses antibiotic treatment as a complementary rather than a comprehensive treatment.

"In public health we are about creating change, not ending disease," he said. "This entails preparation for change within a community. In this case the community is the hospital. What are their cleanliness procedures? Isolation strategies? Waste disposal procedures? Is their objective an MRSA-free situation? What is the cost/benefit analysis of preparation compared with increased medical costs caused by infection?"

He summons precedent to illustrate the second part of the Center's preparedness objective, the breakdown of epidemics into stages or phases. In 1976, the federal government heeded the advice of a group of researchers who accurately believed that influenza moves in cycles but wrongly predicted an imminent cycle because of faulty analysis. The federal government appropriated $137 million to develop a vaccine that had a debilitating side effect, and waited for the assault. Nothing happened: the flu did not materialize.

In contrast, Dr. Taylor cites HIV as an example of a collective failure within the public health community to act quickly enough. In particular, political interference in public health strategy impeded proper preparation of a solution and the methodical education and preparation of the affected communities.

"Experts and officials were very late in setting a clear objective," Henry said.

He went on to note: "You don't want to be too early or too late because the political and fiscal authorities will remind you the next time and not fund a sufficient response. Dr. Charles Chapin, a godfather of public health, believed that you don't go to politicians when an event is just starting, but rather when you are in crisis mode. You go when the outbreak is in full swing and make your pitch for investment at that time. It is a rather manipulative tenet, but a necessary one. It is the nature of our business, and Chapin revolutionized it in the early part of the twentieth century."

The World Health Organization prescribes a six-phase pandemic assessment and reaction process. For each phase, the objectives are very different. The CDC now thinks of epidemics like hurricanes with categories of severity.

Henry believes that public health depends upon adhering to these methodical processes as the objectives of preparation.

This view leads him directly to the topic of the potential avian flu pandemic.

"Different animals get different versions of a disease, and the reason avian flu stalled in the 2006–07 winter is because it is hard for the viruses to jump into the human biological system," Henry said. "But in time, a new human virus will develop. We know it will happen eventually from public health precedents. Our objective has to be to act on the best evidence without panicking. We are doing a fair job at that now, but not a perfect one."

As another example of the poor use of phasing to inform strategy, Henry notes that the costly vaccines being developed in 2007 may not be adequate or sufficient by the time the avian flu virus fully translates to a new human virus.

"We set our objective of needing a vaccine, but some companies are producing it based on the best available sample of the virus, and that won't be the best vaccine when the virus makes the full jump to humans," he said. "At that time our objective will be more specific. While we can develop the factories and methods now, we should invest the most in vaccine development at phase 4 when the sample is superior and closer to what we will really face as a population."

Instead, Henry would prefer the resources be devoted to community-based preparation like education of citizens and of medical personnel, creation of community-based task forces and health departments, and the construction of a network for public health communications.

"You anticipate a certain situation based on precedents and investigation, and your specific response will come out of that preparation," Henry said. "The underlying objective is always the same—the maintenance and improvement of public health. The commitment to method is key. Rushing or overreacting based on alarm or political pressure undermines our preparation."

The enormity of these challenges is matched by the complexity of the cellular world. Clear objectives offer Henry and his colleagues the best chance of tracking and controlling unwelcome visitations from the microbial world. Objectives in Henry's high-stakes field are only potent when they are clearly established and diligently pursued.

REPEAT, REPEAT, REPEAT

Michelle Shepherd

One of the critical parts of any manager's job is getting people to collaborate and form an effective team. It is always a challenge, but especially so in a large company.

Michelle Shepherd, executive of the East Division of Bank of America, uses clear objectives as the way to meet that challenge. Her success shows that defining and repeating objectives makes all the difference in building a motivated and cohesive team.

Michelle has four very specific objectives that she is constantly stating and monitoring: (1) driving material increases in sales each fiscal year; (2) improving what she calls "customer delight" at each bank branch to a score of 9 or 10 on a scale of 10; (3) completely complying with banking regulations; and (4) constantly improving employee satisfaction.

The fulfillment of these four objectives consumes Michelle. They are the mental outline she uses to structure her day. Everyone, from her leadership team to tellers at far-flung Bank of America branches, knows what they are. The clarity of her commitment to these objectives is obvious and contagious. They are her team's refrain, and the growth of her East Division is a reflection of the clarity with which Michelle defines them.

Michelle came up through the ranks at credit card giant MBNA before it was bought by Bank of America to gain access to MBNA's vast and lucrative credit card business. Michelle had been instrumental in MBNA's innovation and success with its card sponsorship program. An added benefit of the acquisition was MBNA's entrepreneurial and innovative culture.

"One of my primary means of achieving our four objectives is bringing a more entrepreneurial approach to the way we see things and do things," Michelle said. "Banking is not a business you usually associate with entrepreneurship but, from the way we deal with customers and innovations at the branch level, there is a huge role for entrepreneurship."

Entrepreneurs are intensely devoted to their objectives because the stakes are so high for them. Michelle's encouragement of an entrepreneurial attitude at a large bank helps instill the common drive to achieve her four objectives. The repetition of these four clear goals helps the people in a large organization develop a common mission. The clarity and simplicity of four objectives that transcend department or position give a big group a nimbleness and focus.

"Every week on Monday at 8 A.M., I evaluate these four factors with my leadership team," Michelle said. "It can sometimes get frustrating, but repetition is a very powerful technique. We live and breathe our four objectives."

Although she may sound like a broken record, Michelle knows that the success her team enjoys from sharing and pursuing these objectives will minimize any frustration they will feel with the constant repetition.

Michelle uses her refrain to focus a team on what is important in a large organization, to provide a common language, and to help develop a common theme and brand. When so many people are working on so many different tasks at a large institution like Bank of America, coherence and teamwork result from the constant reinforcement of common goals.

"If you develop a common approach for an entire team to go about their work, it is likely that the work will yield better results and be more organized," Michelle said. "So if we want to achieve our four objectives, I try to lead, coach, and manage my people with them clearly in mind."

Michelle has an expression I love: "Be kind to people, but be cruel to time." That summarizes how she approaches coaching the employees of her bank into keeping their eyes on their four main objectives.

She is as kind a coach as they come—I see her with a genuine interest in the professional advancement and skill development of her team. But she teaches a system in a way that reminds me of Eric Mangini's work with the Jets. Both Michelle and Eric insist on methodical preparation because it maximizes the productive use of time. In each of their businesses, time is an even scarcer resource than talent.

Michelle shows how great coaches emphasize repetition of objectives. In fact, be it at a bank or on the field, what may seem irritating at first to players or staff can become a reliable and welcome system.

KEY POINTS

OBJECTIVES

- Understanding your objectives requires that you slow down and ask: What and why? What am I doing and why am I doing it?

- The clarity that results from the answers to these questions guides your next preparation steps, helps you see links with other tasks or goals, and keeps you from relying on impulse or intuition.

- Purpose-driven work leads to superior performance, and this principle emphasizes the importance of establishing a clear purpose before doing anything else.

- Steve Bisciotti shows how a clear and aggressive definition of objectives is the cornerstone of preparation. Steve sets his objectives and never blinks as he pursues them.

- Dr. Henry Taylor demonstrates the way in which objectives can be broken down into components to better understand and communicate them.

- Michelle Shepherd illustrates how the constant and clear repetition of objectives can become a key way to build a team's morale and focus.

4

SOMEONE, SOMEWHERE HAS PROBABLY DONE THIS BEFORE

Plan with Precedents

Examining precedents helps you uncover what has been done before in similar situations to help you meet present challenges. Precedents may include common steps or shrewd maneuvers, logical decisions or risky bets, strategies or strokes of luck, prompt or last-minute adjustments, great achievements or simple mistakes from the arc of your career, from other people, or even from the grand stage of history itself.

If you are a lawyer, you know that there are binding

precedents and persuasive precedents in court cases. Binding precedents are imposed on lower courts by higher courts. In business, or life for that matter, precedents are rarely binding but can often be persuasive.

Planning with precedents requires you to be an amateur historian, a detective, and a hobbyist all in one. Precedents should persuade you one way or the other about how to forecast alternative outcomes and develop a strategy.

For example, you may face a situation in which a competitor is undercutting your pricing for a service or product. Because dropping your price is not an alternative, you look for transactions in which you or others have successfully warded off pricing challenges. You uncover instances in which your competitor failed to meet promised distribution times, a factor important to your customers. You make guaranteed delivery dates a key part of your deals instead of reducing prices. Your customers are convinced and you fight off the pricing threat.

On a larger scale, had the United States paid more attention to the dismal precedent of France in Indochina, it is possible that the Vietnam quagmire would not have occurred and the spread of communism would have been dealt with more effectively and with less bloodshed. Indeed, it is shocking how rarely military leaders seem to consider the failures of previous invasions or attacks. I don't know enough about the history of Iraq to comprehend what led to such a breakdown in the construction of a civil society there. But some mix of political, military, and intelligence leaders must have failed to fully heed the failures of similar efforts.

This is not to advocate a blind devotion to the past. The rapidly changing nature of contemporary business and life may make knowledge of previous events less relevant, or sometimes irrelevant. Take debt, for example: your parents may have warned you about it, but accumulating reasonable debt may not be such a bad thing for a company or a household. A generation ago, careers played out at one or two companies. Today, switching companies regularly instead of growing within an organization may benefit your career. So using precedents well means identifying the fundamental preparation pattern from similar projects that you can apply to the current task.

Credible precedents are also tools for persuading others about a point of view or strategy. I love to draw lessons from biographies, history books, or film and apply them to my personal and business situations. For example, *The Wind That Shakes the Barley* is a moving film about the fight for Irish independence from England in the first part of the twentieth century. The film dramatized a range of leadership errors made by the British and the Irish opposition leaders in rural towns. The grassroots errors of the local Irish Republican Army were particularly vivid. Two brothers split over a failure to clearly and persuasively articulate their objectives for a free Ireland. The leaders allowed emotion and innuendo to derail efforts to educate their fellow citizens. The pros and cons of a hard-line, get-out-now or a more conciliatory, gradual approach to the British were never clearly and calmly debated. Both sides on the Irish debate lost their focus on the ultimate objective: a free Ireland.

Fratricide resulted as men and women who thought the treaty to be too conciliatory toward the British turned against the treaty makers and their numerous Irish supporters. The assassination of the great Irish leader Michael Collins symbolized the madness of this civil war. The film's portrayal of a historical precedent provided me with a persuasive example for clearly articulating objectives and redirecting leaders prone to emotional resolution of contentious problems.

The use of precedents applies to both you and your counterpart. That is, you should examine precedents that inform your situation as well as those that may support or strengthen the position of the other side in a deal or negotiation. Imagine yourself the historian of your type of business situation. Gather as best you can the histories that affect, inform, and empower both you and your audience or adversary. You can walk into your presentation or meeting with the force of history behind you. As Oliver Wendell Holmes said, "An ounce of history is worth a pound of logic."

LOTS OF HAIR

Early in my legal career, that unforgettable American musical and cultural moment called *Hair* came to Baltimore. Baltimore is a charming city, but slightly more conservative than New York. Or, at the time, let's say a bit more than slightly. Just as I was building a law practice, getting involved with politics, and starting to work with Orioles players, I was faced with the delicate challenge of representing the controversial musical, prior to its opening, against the strident challenges it faced from some ultra-conservative and religious groups in town. I have tried to never champion one point of view without considering all the others, so I wanted to represent *Hair* in a way that recognized all points of view while respecting the First Amendment rights of the producer, actors, and audience.

Hair had already played in a few cities other than New York. The nudity onstage was making headlines nationally and arousing ire locally. I had no special commitment to the show or to public nudity, but I did love the challenge of my first big First Amendment case. So I embraced the value of precedents, both legal and historical, and there began my commitment to a concept that grew into the second principle—precedents—on the Preparation Principles Checklist.

Two kinds of precedents were relevant here: the traditional legal ones as well as the contemporaneous precedents of what had played out in other cities prior to the arrival of *Hair* in Baltimore. So first my colleagues and I drafted a concise opinion for the producers of *Hair* on why the display of the human body in those various scenes was a constitutionally protected expression. But we were very careful to analyze the strategies of other lawyers in other cities. In particular, we focused on how these lawyers presented the case to the public as much as to the courts. And we also focused on the strategies and arguments of lawyers representing those advocating the censorship or halt of the shows.

The idea was to pick the language and presentations from these precedents that would best work to appease public opinion in Baltimore while simultaneously making a strong legal case. We used these precedents, in a sense, as persuaders—the show went on and the actors and actresses performed their scene in the buff. Good precedents persuade you how to deal or negotiate, and they also persuade your audience to listen more closely and possibly even accept an approximation of your proposed terms.

Precedents hold an impressive ability to convince. So you likewise have to be careful not to grasp for or cling to precedents as automatic justifications. It reminds me of that old high school lesson about how correlation is not necessarily causation. Precedents can hold such an uncanny power to convince that audiences very often grab onto them without scrutinizing their relevance or their applicability. When precedents are presented clearly and artfully, they become problem solvers, since many of us are almost wired to accept the power of history and of previous examples. They are very useful preparation tools for clarifying issues and an appropriate course of action.

TALKING A FRIEND BACK TO FINANCIAL REALITY

A well-known professional sports general manager called me one evening. His team was in the middle of a hugely successful playoff run. He was the toast of the game and the national press. He was not only immersed in the day-to-day operations of his club, but also pleased by the growth of his own value in the executive marketplace. He maintained an external modesty, but you could tell that he was running the risk of overpricing his contract value because of his role in the team's turnaround.

Not surprisingly, he was calling to seek advice about negotiating a new contract for himself as soon as the season ended. And I immediately realized a case as common in the business of sports as in the business world at large. There was no way an owner or a board of directors or a president would give this fellow the money he thought he deserved. So how do you talk a client or a friend down from his or her financial heights? Well, you use precedents.

So I advised this general manager to caucus his network for contractual precedents; to research them; to brainstorm with his very impressive mind. He may have come up with one or two examples to support his self-image. But I was almost certain that he was intelligent enough to learn from his study of contract precedents both how they might be distinguished and how they might be used against him. He would see that he needed to adjust his goals to stay in the contract ballpark.

In a sense, business is built on precedents—from salaries to mergers and acquisitions. The determination of value—with anomalies like the Internet phenomenon or the ten-year, $250 million contract the Texas Rangers gave to Alex Rodriguez—is based on previous determinations of value. Surpassing previous values or prices requires the assembly of historic and current examples that help rationalize a higher point of agreement.

In this chapter, I look at three people who make precedents a fundamental part of their preparation. Money manager Bill Miller uses precedents from prior investments and historical patterns to determine when to buy or sell big positions in stocks. Firefighter Ann Marie Tierney uses a clearly estab-lished set of precedents to keep herself and her team out of harm's way. And the late journalist and critic Johnny Apple shows that the unlikeliest precedent—be it a meal on another continent or a diplomatic treaty decades ago—can inform a seemingly unrelated story. The fact that precedents are so valuable to people in such diverse fields is the best illustration of their value. And it is not surprising to me that these master preparers are devotees of history. Books on history and biographies sit by their bedsides, fit into their briefcases, and rest on their laps during downtime on airplanes.

Precedents are all about history, and you can learn from the history of your career or the history of certain types of deals or companies in the same way you learn from the great books.

AN UNPRECEDENTED MONEY MANAGER

Bill Miller

Few people in the financial world can claim the accomplishments of Bill Miller. Maybe that is because so few money managers prepare with precedents as devotedly as Bill.

On Halloween 2005, Bill Miller arrived at the office dressed as an oil sheik. He was one of the few famous mutual fund managers who didn't buy into that year's run-up in energy stocks; as a result, he nearly lost his record streak of fifteen years straight beating the return on the S&P 500; he spoofed himself that Halloween and ended up beating the S&P by the end of the Roman calendar year anyway.

On Halloween 2006, I sat with Bill Miller in a conference room at Legg Mason overlooking Baltimore's harbor. He was dressed as what he called a "money pimp." Green shirt, long chains, polyester pants. His staff matched his thoroughly prepared outfitting—tennis stars, debutantes, and Evel Knievel roamed the halls. A lot of preparation goes into Bill Miller's Halloween parties.

His staff that day was also celebrating Bill's twenty-five years at Legg Mason. In addition to hanging out with cutting-edge scientists as chairman of the Santa Fe Institute in his spare time, Bill runs Legg Mason Value Trust fund and is the chairman of Legg Mason Capital Management. Altogether, he oversees more than $50 billion in capital that large and small investors pour into his hands to try to make better lives for themselves.

When Bill starts talking about preparation, he throws three quotes at you.

First comes Ben Franklin: By failing to prepare, you are preparing to fail. I thought legendary UCLA basketball coach John Wooden said it. Bill clarified the origins of the quote by tying it back to Ben.

Next: It is not practice that makes perfect; it is perfect practice that makes perfect.

Third: Average people practice until they can win; professionals practice until they can't lose.

Bill did a lot of research for this conversation about preparation. And what is most striking is the utter lack of self-seriousness with which he discusses his preparation method and his career. Bill has fun preparing. I imagine the insouciant Ben Franklin did, too. Those of you who equate preparation with drudgery or hoop jumping ought to have the good fortune to work for Bill Miller.

Bill's most impressive preparation skill is his use of precedents. He applies precedents to setting the pattern of his day, to his hiring and assignment of staff, and most important, to his stock picking. He is regularly thinking through the previous event or decision that might inform the current dilemma.

"Precedents by their nature involve an analysis of your prior behaviors or of someone else's," Bill said. "I really spend my day doing that: analyzing investor behavior, analyzing a company's behavior, analyzing my own tendencies and previous decisions."

A day in the life of Bill Miller is pretty set in stone these days. He has been picking stocks for nearly three decades, and he has obviously looked at his own patterns and settled on a daily format that produces the best results.

"You have to follow a pattern to make sure you are on top of events that are affecting each of the companies in your portfolio," Bill explained. "I wake up and check the overseas markets, the major news items, changes in currency rates overnight. From there I go to the newspapers and Bloomberg and the wires. Then the markets open and I try to get a sense of how our positions are behaving that day. Then I do my e-mail. Then I go into the office around 1 P.M. I hold this pattern because I can get more done in the morning alone and I couldn't prepare in the office because I would keep getting interrupted."

Bill has analyzed his own routines to determine the best pattern for his day and for his staff. He lets them work in peace in the morning on their research and correspondence and presentations. Then in the afternoon they get together and collaborate.

"This pattern is my preparation template on a daily basis," Bill said. "It is all a system that has been refined with practice into a seven-day-a-week pattern."

As far as hiring his well-respected team of analysts and traders, Bill essentially uses himself as an example.

"I am not extremely orderly," he said with a laugh. "And

my analysis of myself got me interested in social psychology and behavioral psychology. We have a psychologist do personality assessments during our analyst training to identify the personality styles and types here. Preparation will play a different role for each person depending on the personality type."

The application of his own self-awareness to his staffing and training techniques is a simple but innovative use of precedents. Bill knows himself—his strengths, weaknesses, intellectual interests, and personal convictions—as thoroughly as any professional I have met. That self-knowledge, and his reading in relevant fields, has led him to a point where he matches personality templates with job profiles.

But Bill does not limit his employment of behavioral psychology to himself and his employees. The study of precedents of market and investor behavior has allowed him to make hugely successful investments at times when financial markets were collapsing and investors were rushing for the exits.

In 2001, when market panic accompanied the terrorist attacks of September 11, Bill and his team maintained their collective cool and profited on irrational panic. The study of previous market crises like the collapse of 1929 and 1987 and a methodical comparison of market conditions with these prior events allowed Miller to determine that the crisis did not merit its market reaction.

Bill called his use of precedents and social and behavioral psychology one of his fund's "competitive advantages."

"Investors overweight dramatic events," he said. "After 9/11, we bought immediately. In 1987, we determined that the crash was a liquidity implosion, not a failing economy. If liquidity were put back in, the economy and market would be fine. Instead of just acting, we looked at economic conditions during similar events and made our decisions accordingly."

As for specific stock selection, Bill likewise uses precedents from his own portfolio but also from other disciplines.

In the case of his highly successful investment in the Google initial public offering in 2004, Bill reached out to academia to master the complexities of auction theory. Google structured its IPO as more of an auction than the typical IPO in which an offering price is set and a fixed number of shares are offered for investors to purchase. So Bill sought out an expert in auction theory at the California Institute of Technology. The professor explained the mechanics and nuances of auctions to Bill, preparing him to determine appropriate bid prices and strategy for the investment.

Bill assembled a sort of Google task force: one member of his team focused on Google's long-term growth strategy; another focused on the economics of search engines; a third studied its financial modeling and forecasting. Together they determined that Google's opportunity for growth was substantial and that the auction afforded an opportunity to amass a large amount of shares at a discount to intrinsic value.

The task force determined that the poor reception of the Google IPO by the news media was a knee-jerk reaction prompted by Google's unwillingness to provide a large amount of information to investors, their inclusion of a less than shareholder friendly governance schedule, and their timing of the IPO in the summertime. Also, Google minimized the role of investment banks by structuring the deal as an auction so banks could not guarantee a certain number of shares to their best clients.

"Our determination, primarily from our conversations

with the auction theorist, was that there was a big opportunity here if we were willing to sit down and work through it," Bill said. "We also analyzed another precedent in that we already owned Amazon, eBay, and Yahoo. But we were most reassured by the auction theorist who seemed assured that the structure of the auction would allow you to bid what you thought the stock was worth and expect that return. We went into this extremely well prepared and thought that few others would be taking such a big risk."

The study of specific stock-picking examples, past economic events and trends, and comparables from other fields has contributed to a stunning return for Bill's shareholders at the fund. He has set a precedent in his industry in large part because of his own unique but methodical preparation.

THE PRECEDENTS OF FIRE

Ann Marie Tierney

In certain jobs, failure to prepare with precedents can get you killed.

Ann Marie Tierney works for Firestorm Wildland Fire Suppression, a company based in Chico, California. She spends fourteen days in a row in forests and national parks. Sometimes she is fighting controlled fires that the Forest Service or park service set intentionally. Sometimes she and her colleagues are trying to beat back wildfires to save towns and lives.

Ann's story shows that using precedents entails not simply compiling a list but also judiciously applying it to the challenge of the moment. Ann must quickly select from an established list of eighteen precedents that apply to a sudden crisis caused by raging fire. To use the legal analogy, these are not persuasive but binding precedents. In some jobs, the past is a completely reliable predictor of the future.

On October 2, 2004, Ann and her crew were fighting a fire on government land in the Sequoia Kings National Park in California. It was a "controlled burn"—essentially a "prescription" fire where the National Park Service hires Ann's company to burn off sections of a forest. The objective is to control forest growth and revitalize the forests.

A treetop in the prescribed area caught fire when the wind carried sparks upward. Some in Ann's group assembled below the tree to discuss cutting it down because they feared that the tree would fall on them while they were working nearby.

Unfortunately, that fear was realized. A six-foot-long piece of the treetop cracked off and clobbered a firefighter. The impact was so strong that he was partially buried in the ground.

"Precedents didn't fail us," Ann said. "It was our negligence. There is a clear precedent not to stand under a leaning tree that is on fire. They stood by the tree for about twenty minutes discussing their strategy. We were telling them to move. Most of us heeded precedent. The guy who didn't got killed."

In the firefighting business, you catch what they call "fire fever." These people have a passion for fighting fires, for understanding fire, for being around it. Its beauty and heat, the outdoors and hard work all attract them.

But they manage their passion with a method. In the wildfire business, there are what professionals call the "10s and 18s." The 10s are standard firefighting orders. You obey them at all costs; you obey them to stay alive.

The 18s are called "watch-out situations." They are essentially precedents that forest firefighters have seen enough to know that they will see them again. They include mistakes in judgment and communication, as well as uncontrollable weather situations. It is worth listing them in their entirety here:

1. Fire not scouted and sized up.

2. In country not seen in daylight.

3. Safety zones and escape routes not identified.

4. Unfamiliar with weather and local factors influencing fire behavior.

5. Uninformed on strategy, tactics, and hazards.

6. Instructions and assignments not clear.

7. No communication link with crew members/supervisor.

8. Constructing fire line without safe anchor point.

9. Building fire line downhill with fire below.

10. Attempting frontal assault on fire.

11. Unburned fuel between you and the fire.

12. Cannot see main fire, not in contact with anyone who can.

13. On a hillside where rolling material can ignite fuel below.

14. Weather is getting hotter and drier.

15. Wind increases and/or changes direction.

16. Getting frequent spot fires across line.

17. Terrain and fuels make escape to safety zones difficult.

18. Taking a nap near the fire line.

The amazing thing about these precedents is how current they are. They are simple, seemingly obvious, and nevertheless a matter of life and death. Ann and her team likely see several of them on every trip into the forest.

"I am not sure how they were narrowed down to eighteen," Ann said. "But these are the mistakes and events you tend to see. Even the behavior of fire can be narrowed down."

Even fire, as wild and fierce as it is, can be largely controlled with proper preparation.

Ann points to precedent number 16, spot fires, as one of the most frequent and dangerous situations that she invariably faces. Her team usually uses the technique of drawing a line and maintaining it as the "no-go zone" for the fire. Every effort is made to contain the wildfire behind that line. Essentially, success means that the fire is no longer wild— its containment is the first step toward its elimination.

And in the case of controlled burns, the line is the fundamental premise of that control.

"With a controlled fire, we cut a line so fire can burn up to it but not beyond it," Ann said. "But embers carry and will ignite, especially if humidity is low and there is natural fuel on the ground. Sometimes it happens right in front of me. You have to run and cut right in front of it before it expands.

And at the same time you have to still identify your safe zone."

So at any one moment, Ann is cutting a line around the spot fire, keeping an eye on her safety zone, and communicating with her team about the conditions of the immediate environment.

Fire can creep or it can go crazy. Wind is usually responsible for the latter. Precedent number 15, "wind increases and/or changes direction," also seems to state the obvious. We all know that wind seems to have its own mind. But the fact that the team makes this a formal precedent is not stating the obvious. It is respecting the awesome way in which wind and fire go crazy together.

"Wind makes for the most life-threatening situations," Ann said. "I have had to run through fire before. You get delirious with the intensity of the heat and the smoke."

But because of an adherence to precedent numbers 5 (uninformed on strategy, tactics, and hazards), 6 (instructions and assignments not clear), and 7 (no communication link), Ann knows that running through fire is the proper thing to do. The warning in number 7, to maintain a constant communication link, is the critical piece. If a teammate tells Ann to run through fire, she heeds their command.

"Because of our communication, we are usually told when the wind is coming," Ann said. "We know it is just a wall of fire and not the whole blaze. So in this case you rely on someone else to tell you where to find your safety zone."

The capacity to keep all the precedents in your head at once is the challenge. There are two impediments to that: exhaustion and complacency. The death of Ann's colleague when the treetop fell on him may have been a case of complacency.

Prior to being assigned to this controlled burn, the fire-fighters had been working for several days. They were lulled by a placid spot in the forest. The burning treetop seemed to be the only immediate issue. Moments of peace can provide the pause during which the sheer beauty of fire and the outdoors can seduce the team into complacency.

And so a few of the team forgot the precedents and one man died because of it. "Most of us knew where we needed to be and went there," Ann said. "But in the field you can easily lose track of safety avenues built on precedents. We were devastated. We had to have meetings after that, safety briefings, and get our heads picked at. We turned it into a vivid precedent, though. If I see a crown fire now, I will never forget that this is a watch-out situation."

Ann is as consumed with precedents as she is with fire itself. She realizes that one day sooner or later one of the 18s will save her life. The lesson of Ann Marie Tierney is that, whether a life is at stake or a deal is on the line, preparation with precedents requires that you understand how to apply them once you've compiled them.

A PRECEDENTIAL MAN

R. W. Apple Jr.

R. W. "Johnny" Apple Jr. was a *New York Times* foreign correspondent, bureau chief in such places as Saigon, London, and Washington, D.C., and an acclaimed travel and food writer. He was a big man with a bunch of big jobs.

He described the "Q-head," the name for an analytical story that can appear on page one of the *New York Times* to

help make sense of a momentous event, as "a place to inter-
pret but not opine." Johnny was the Pavarotti of Q-heads. It
is the piece where, as Johnny said, you tell "why it happened and what the consequences might be." As opposed to
an editorial, which prescribes "what ought to be done about
it," or basic reporting, which simply tells "what happened,"
the Q-head is all about the connections among events and
actors and their historical context.

Johnny was all about connections and context, and he
was a legend not least for his ability to write the challenging Q-head. He was also a man of impressive appetites,
and his passion for precedents of all sorts—links between
wars separated by centuries or between wines from different regions—brought better context to stories as disparate
as his coverage of the Biafra crisis or a crab feast in
Baltimore.

My coauthor Greg and I were supposed to meet Johnny to
discuss preparation the day he died in October 2006. A
native of Akron, Ohio, he was eager to talk about the Cleveland Indians, the club my son Mark serves as general
manager. The only direct quote we got from Johnny regarding
precedents came on the phone a few weeks before when he
agreed to be profiled in this book.

"Precedents, well, you have to live a lot and read a lot,"
Johnny said with a laugh.

But a lecture he gave in 2005 on Q-heads and other
endeavors from his "long and shout-filled career," and bountiful insights from former colleagues and friends, tell you a
lot about how Johnny mined and maintained precedents to
establish connections and provide context for the war, meal,
or politician's speech he was analyzing. His approach offers

a lesson in using precedents as an organizing principle for critical analysis.

"Q probably stood for 'queer,'" Johnny said in the lecture, referring to the oddness of the genre when it first started to appear in the paper. The news analysis piece is a relatively new concoction for newspapers. The Q-head evolved, Johnny believed, as newspapers took on some of the role of news-magazines for readers. Newspapers began to realize that not only did we want the facts when we picked up the paper in the morning, but we wanted to know their implications.

Schooled as a reporter, and mindful of the precedents provided for his career by hardscrabble mentors in the 1960s at the *Times*, Johnny probably could never stray far enough from his original calling to be able to write an editorial. Yet, his analytical mind, craving for history, and booming voice (be it in his writing or speaking!) made him the perfect match for the Q-head.

"You are really out there on the wire," Johnny said in his lecture about meeting the deadline and accuracy demands of this peculiar journalistic art form. "You have to get it done, but make it good and make it right."

How Johnny managed to do all three, despite occasional doubts from editors that he would be able to file his Q-head on time, is a tribute as much to his organizational skills as his powerful memory.

For example, when the Senate rejected the Comprehensive Test Ban Treaty in 1999, Johnny was called at six in the evening by editor Andrew Rosenthal to write a sweeping analysis that captured the sweep of what Rosenthal called a "not since Versailles" type of event. Calvin Trillin described what transpired in his 2003 profile of Johnny in the *New Yorker*:

Apple, pointing out that his stepdaughter's rehearsal dinner was to take place at seven-thirty, berated Rosenthal for making such a request at such a time, and, an hour later, filed a Q-head. It was written in clear English. It had historical references to SALT II and the Panama Canal treaties and the tension between Woodrow Wilson and Henry Cabot Lodge during the formation of the League of Nations. It was one thousand one hundred and seventy-one words long. Eleven of those words were, like a tip of the hat to Rosenthal, "Not since the Versailles Treaty was voted down in November 1919 . . ."

Eric Schmitt, a former colleague at the *Times*, saw Johnny's ability to summon precedents in the heat of battle during the first Iraq war. "Johnny was a notorious deadline filer, pushing copy until the very last moment," Eric said. "Editors would be pulling their hair out, calling for copy. He'd reach into his piles and pull out just the right pool report he wanted. Or lean over and grab a reference book from the floor, to cite some military precedent. He was an avid reader and student of history—drawing comparisons with campaigns in the Civil War, WWI, and WWII, as well as his own experience in Vietnam."

Eric fondly recalls that Johnny would summon precedents not only to bolster his stories, but also to buck up young writers: "The 1991 Persian Gulf War was the first time I'd worked with Johnny. I struggled at first to gain some traction in carving out my own niche. But one day Apple gave me a spectacular piece of advice. 'The best way to get inside the high command'—one of my stated assignments as the resident Pentagon correspondent on the ground—'is to write about them. Why don't you write a series of short profiles on the half dozen or so top officers running this war, particularly those readers may not have heard of? You write even a short piece about them and they're flattered. They'll take your call again on other subjects.' It was a technique he'd used in Vietnam to get acquainted with the top brass there, and it paid off in spades for me, and for the paper. Two of the profilees, in particular, became crucial sources for several exclusive pieces."

In a sense, Johnny's years as a foreign correspondent provided the precedent for what he did best and loved most toward the end of his career—writing about travel and food. His stories of meals and journeys were rich with comparisons from his own previous trips, associations with food from different continents, and recollections of former dining companions.

Todd Purdum, Johnny's close friend and former colleague, was one of the people who helped review Johnny's food and travel files after his death. Archaeology seems to have been the apt metaphor for the system of compiling precedents.

"His filing system helped him easily find a relevant event if he could not readily recall some parallel," Todd said. "For his travel and food files, every folder he kept was multilayered. Guidebooks, classic books from the area of the story, often a work or two of literature from an area's dominant author or poet, clippings—it was all like a piece of rock formation."

Alice Waters, chef and owner of Chez Panisse in Berkeley, California, spoke at Johnny's memorial service, saying he illustrated the "connection between commitment and contentment."

To twist her words, Johnny found much contentment in his commitment to connections—to precedents across time, genres, and geography. For Alice, that led to his understanding that food is a political and cultural phenomenon.

"There seems to be a concept in journalism and in life for that matter that you have to confine your expertise," Alice said. "Johnny refused that. His writing linked so many fields and events together because his years of reporting and traveling showed him that this was the case. He understood the bigger politics of food like no other."

Indeed, Alice sees Johnny's love of food as part and parcel of an insatiable inquisitiveness.

"His smell was fine-tuned, his eyes, his ears, he picked up everything through this palette and took in information a little bit like a wild animal who needs it for its survival," Alice said. "His awareness of everything around him allowed him to absorb information and use it for that story or years later."

Johnny Apple shows that precedents can provide a foundation for a more precise way to think. Be it in writing, cooking, or public speaking, his approach showed how to produce a livelier and more comprehensive presentation of a story.

KEY POINTS

PRECEDENTS

- The past is prologue—the maxim applies to almost any endeavor. You can methodically analyze past experiences to shape your preparation for current and future undertakings.

- Planning with precedents can be enriching when you look to other fields and even historical figures for comparables. Once you have defined your objectives, it helps to think about books you have read, people you have worked with, or even movies you have seen to trigger informative analogies.

- Precedents are great persuaders that can be used to make presentations, pitches, and negotiations more forceful.

- Bill Miller bases his incomparable system of stock picking on studying market and company precedents. He is a master at thinking outside the box—drawing historical patterns and ideas from wide-ranging fields and figures to support his decisions.

- Ann Marie Tierney shows precedents at their most fundamental level in fire fighting. Her system of precedents shapes every move she makes to achieve her objective of safely putting out a fire.

- R. W. Apple shows how precedents strengthen your point and enrich your presentation. His lively use of them in journalism is an example for almost any written or oral presentation you make.

5

WHAT'S IN THE FORECAST?

Know the Alternatives

Precedents help you prepare by looking backward. By knowing your alternatives, you look forward and try to forecast potential results that will range from the least desired to one that completely fulfills your goal. Be it in hiring a new employee or investing in a stock, in starting a company or selling one, in public speaking or board presentations, forecasting your alternative endgames helps guide you down the correct path.

Unless you understand fully what your potential outcomes may be, it is hard to come to a conclusion about the steps you should take to achieve the best result. For example, in negotiation, it is crucial that you establish both your highest goal and walk-away alternatives. That is, what is the best price, highest amount, best deal structure that you are seeking? And, to the contrary, at what point do you walk away from the table when you see that you cannot even come close to an acceptable outcome? In a negotiation you try to get something from the other side. You analyze their potential leverage in dealing with you by understanding outcomes they may want to achieve as well as your own. Can either of you afford to overask? To play hardball? To walk away from the table without getting a deal done?

Or, if you are considering a new job, you have to analyze your options in several contexts. What is an alternative to that new job? Can you remain in your existing position and perhaps improve the situation? Should you try to make some adjustments and wait it out a bit longer? The issue, in this and most other cases, becomes whether alternatives are realistically achievable.

When considering a new job offer, you also have to analyze your prospective employer's alternatives. What alternatives does she have to hiring you? How realistic are they? Whom might she hire other than you? The second dimension of alternatives is projecting the other party's outcomes.

Forecasting alternative outcomes will increase the likelihood that you will structure a strategy that helps attain the most desired result. You are imagining the various ends before you establish your means. And you are identifying the potential outcome that will most closely satisfy your objectives.

By setting the parameters of your results, you focus yourself in a way that helps you set a clear strategy.

ALTERNATIVE OFFERS

I realized the value of a methodical compilation of alternatives when I recently consulted with a medium-sized media company in Seattle. Its outstanding growth and overall high level of performance had a downside as its executives became targets for hiring by larger New York– and Los Angeles–based firms with "deep pockets" and the ability to lure top talent with big pay packages. My client's board knew that headhunters were circling Susan, their rising superstar of a COO. If they were successful in wooing her away, it would mean the third executive team loss in two years. She was an incredibly talented and charismatic leader, and there was no one left internally with the experience to replace her.

My client could budget a salary of $400,000 per year plus some bonuses and perks. It was an attractive offer but in no way would compete with what companies in the media capitals could offer. Offers in this league would certainly tempt many job candidates.

As we prepared to make the offer, we examined alternatives based on precedents of comparable pay packages at companies in similarly high quality-of-life cities like Portland, Oregon, and Denver, Colorado. We constructed several other alternative outcomes. One was at $400,000 a year and included significant bonuses for performance. The other was at a high salary of $500,000 a year but with slightly lower bonuses. The latter was our walk-away point, meaning that we would go no higher even if it meant losing Susan to the competition.

As we reviewed the New York and Los Angeles alternatives for Susan, we came to realize that while we couldn't match the dollars, they couldn't satisfy the advantage we had in Seattle with family living close by, a beautiful vacation home on the water, and a more reasonable cost of living. Based on her lifestyle interests, we felt we could ultimately construct a strategy focused on balancing the COO's life-style choices and compensation. Her lifestyle would be superior to what she might attain in the major markets.

In essence, we forecast our alternative outcomes by ana-lyzing hers. The development of alternative outcomes, in-formed by a study of precedents and Susan's interests, led our client to develop a better strategy for retaining its COO. She stayed, the company thrives, and, based on the incen-tives in her package and relative buying power in Seattle, she is making nearly as much money as she would with her woo-ers and enjoying the quality of life she has always sought.

MY MINI MIDLIFE CRISIS

One morning in the winter of 1992 my wife, Cathi, and I took a walk on a beautiful Caribbean beach. I had reached a point in my life where the practice of law had lost its allure for me. I was suffering from a common case of legal burnout. Being tied to a time sheet had less appeal than ever as my other business ventures were growing. During the walk, we laid out the professional and lifestyle alternatives that I could explore. The most profound thing Cathi said to me was that she noticed how much I loved to teach. Teaching in an academic institution didn't appeal to me since I'm an entrepreneur at heart. We brainstormed other teaching alternatives after look-ing at precedents set by people with similar interests.

Weighing alternative careers allowed me to feel that I could take control of my life. The mere exercise allowed me to understand that I did not have to leave one thing to do another. So a walk on the beach led to my recognition that I could stay associated with my law firm as an adviser, continue with my sports firm, and channel my passion for teaching into the founding of what would become the Shapiro Negotiations Institute. I could then be an entrepreneur, add income and excitement, and complement my other endeavors. Alternative outcomes are not mutually exclusive; sometimes you can set your strategy to attain a result that is a combination of them.

IT'S ALL A STATE OF MIND

I have bad news and good news about forecasting alternatives. The bad news is that sometimes you can't find any valid alternatives and the best thing to do is to stop looking for them.

The good news is that even if you discover no real alternatives, merely going through the exercise can help your state of mind. After assessing precedents and alternatives, you may find that you are stuck. Or you may simply opt for the status quo. Or there may be no good options for proceeding at that moment in time. However, the exercise of running methodically through precedents and alternatives should make it easier for you to cease looking at such a situation or challenge in a negative way.

For example, you may discover that the best alternative is not doing the deal or not making the phone call. It is important to realize that doing nothing is still an alternative. I have found in more than a few transactions that the walk-away alternative not only can help you avoid pursuing a potentially harmful step, but also can lead to new opportunities that you had not contemplated. The methodical approach allows you to find the positives, or at least realize that the negatives may not be as overwhelming as once thought. Method minimizes angst. It gives you a greater sense of control and perspective.

The next three people profiled identify potential outcomes in order to pursue the one that best suits their objectives. Historian Taylor Branch wants his readers to experience a vivid history and not an academic one, so he structures his books to help achieve this outcome. From his career track to his company's acquisitions, Bill Walton compiles and weighs alternatives before making any move. Wine critic Robert Parker selects alternative ways to critique alternative wines in a way that has reinvented an industry.

ALTERNATIVE HISTORY

 *Taylor Branch*

Taylor Branch says: "Preparation is craft." As a historian and as a writer, you see Taylor's craftsmanship in his three-part history of the civil rights movement in America—*Parting the Waters*, *Pillar of Fire*, and *At Canaan's Edge*. His historical tour de force is the product of Taylor's dedication to the outcome of an accessible history driven more by human stories and voices than analysis and theory.

Taylor's craft entails interviewing hundreds of people, distilling thousands of stories into a narrative, and pulling it all off with fine prose. Taylor gives almost anyone in any profession an example of how the analysis of alternative outcomes helps you settle upon a presentation of all the information you have assembled for a presentation.

As a historian, Taylor first had to decide whether he wanted to be a storyteller or an analyzer. As a writer, he had to select from hundreds of alternative stories to illustrate key moments and sustain his historical narrative. And as an interviewer, he had to select from alternative approaches to best summon accurate and lively anecdotes and recollections from the nearly one thousand people he spoke with as part of his research for each of the books.

Analysis of alternatives in each of these three areas is a big part of the reason Taylor Branch is one of our most acclaimed historians.

A HISTORIAN'S ALTERNATIVES

Before he could even begin to analyze how he would tell a story, Taylor had to come to grips with the fundamental alternative that I suppose faces almost every historian: What is the story? What world do I want the reader to enter into?

If anything, the research complicates the clear determination of the story. So much is fascinating; so much seems important. The selection of an alternative can be a paralyzing process.

Taylor developed a complex filing system that had as its labels each month of almost every year since 1790. He built a computer database that cross-referenced events and people. His analysis of whom to include in the narrative and of what events to emphasize became a fundamental part of his preparation. Ultimately, a fundamental decision over how to tell the history facilitated his culling of people and events.

"What crystallized for me during my preparation was one major rule: the deeper I went into the research, the more committed I was to using more storytelling and less analysis," Taylor said. "Most history in the United States is analytical history, particularly in race relations. But by asking people to cross cultural boundaries and to do it with stories and not ideas, we get outside of the categories we use to make us feel comfortable in the world. It became a question not so much of what angle do you tell one story from but what approach to the story delivers the biggest punch to the reader."

A WRITER'S ALTERNATIVES

Once he settled into his structural alternative, Taylor had to determine the best alternatives with which to make the storytelling flow into a cohesive narrative. The first chapter of the first book in the trilogy, *Parting the Waters,* is emblematic of this analysis. Taylor was struggling to find a powerful and suitably metaphoric way to begin such a vast and complicated history. Do you begin where most people would—with Martin Luther King Jr.? Do you begin with a dramatic or tragic incident like a lynching or a march? Taylor analyzed all his alternatives and settled on a lesser known but strikingly charismatic and influential civil rights leader and mentor named Vernon Johns.

"I was ready to start writing, felt I had researched enough, and the opening was really causing major problems for me," Taylor said. "I wanted to communicate this part of our culture through a story and through a person. How do you communicate that right away without writing an essay on the nature of the southern black church? I was stuck. Then

I stumbled on a guy called Vernon Johns, King's predecessor as a minister. In terms of my storytelling, this guy was eccentric and human enough that you could tell his story and still have readers absorb the critical background about the culture of black church that led to King."

At the same time, there were scores of compelling people whom Taylor had to leave out of the story so as not to confound the reader with too many names, digressions, and anecdotes.

For example, *Parting the Waters* is dedicated to Septima Clark, one of Taylor's favorite people in the entire civil rights movement. Yet she didn't make it into any of the books.

"While Septima Clark had the biggest influence on me of any person I interviewed, by my craft rules—storytelling for biggest payoff—I couldn't include her in the narrative. She was always off screen—she wasn't at the big meetings and demonstrations. I would break my own rules if I tried to fit her in. Part of the preparation is determining how and who you fit into the narrative to get the biggest payoff for the reader."

AN INTERVIEWER'S ALTERNATIVES

Taylor was always mindful while conducting his nearly one thousand interviews of the supremacy of the reader's craving for story. But his interviews—every single one—required an objective analysis of alternative outcomes, too. He would study the interviewee's personality and personal history, his or her role in the movement, and his or her need to talk about a certain event, experience, or emotion. Each interview required a different approach based on Taylor's preparation for it. He had to hear each interviewee break through clichés and see his or her small part on history's stage in a new way.

"The whole purpose is to accommodate the person you are talking to and trying to learn something from," Taylor said. "It usually is a good interview if you ask them about their private reality, not the public perception. I used to get what I call the 'Martin increased in stature and favor with God and man and I was his friend' line too often. It was too easy to fall into the trap of saying how virtuous the black guys were and how nasty the sheriff was. So my rule for an interview was the whole movement was about private struggles every day. The real meat of it was people trying to figure out what they were going to do and where they fit in conflict with themselves or within their own circles. I had to do enough research to get to those questions. The preparation was finding those places that got me the most animation, pride, or hesitation."

Again, it is not hard to see how the preparation with alternatives by Taylor Branch is similar to the preparation of anyone involved in a setting that requires interpersonal interaction and probing.

The Reverend Ralph Abernathy surely had answered tens of thousands of questions in his lifetime about Martin Luther King and the civil rights movement. But by discovering Abernathy's admiration for Vernon Johns, Taylor uncovered an alternative way to gain new insight from Abernathy and an energized analysis of the entire movement.

"Nobody had ever asked Abernathy about Vernon Johns," Taylor said. "So by showing your subject that you are trying to break into their world and capture its full reality, and by asking them for something new, you get a whole new discovery. Preparation does that for me."

Similarly, Taylor looked for an alternative way to present

J. Edgar Hoover and fit the FBI director into his story. Instead of bashing his paranoia and narcissism, Taylor decided to take one incident and let it illuminate both the talented bureaucrat and terrible opportunist that was Hoover.

"For me the biggest decision at the beginning of the third book was to focus on this one county in Alabama to show Hoover in a new way," Taylor said. "Nobody had ever heard of Lowndes County—it was 80 percent black, full of sharecroppers, and no black person there had voted in the twentieth century. So I decided that my best alternative was to show Hoover through the place and people he was hurting. Hoover sabotaged the investigation of a Klan murder there. He had an informant there who was murdering and participating in all kinds of Klan stuff. The guy had a free ride and the FBI had no interest in controlling him. He was in the car when they murdered someone. Hoover pitched it to President Johnson that the FBI had miraculously solved the case when he had a guy participating in it."

When he talked about preparation in the interview, Taylor occasionally would rest his head on his hands that were folded on the table. He was processing the alternative ways to answer each question about preparation. When he talked about Hoover, Taylor grew especially animated.

This is when he said the great line, "Preparation is craft." Engaging in a thorough analysis of alternatives is a vital part of that craft. Taylor highlighted for me that, whether you are delivering history or presenting a service or product, having a clear outcome in mind leads to a more convincing and engaging story.

AN ALTERNATIVE MIND

Bill Walton

Bill Walton has that Clint Eastwood look in his eye.

You have probably seen Eastwood in movies and may have heard him talk in interviews about his work as a politician, director, or actor. His public persona and his film characters blur together more than almost anyone in Hollywood.

Walton has that same measured tone, glance, and gait, methodically formulating and assessing his sentences before speaking. The habit of weighing his alternatives seems to be in his DNA.

Whether you are a deal maker or decision maker at any level of any enterprise, the way Bill aggregates and measures his alternatives is both practical and instructive.

Allied Capital, Bill's company, provides debt and equity financing to over 140 private, middle-market companies that generate aggregate revenues of over $13 billion and employ more than ninety thousand people. It offers investors the opportunity to participate in the U.S. private equity industry through an investment in publicly traded stock. Bill's preoccupation with alternatives significantly contributed to his company's delivery of a ten-year average annual return to shareholders of 18 percent through the end of 2006.

"A key to preparation is your temperament," Bill said. "Our business is basically about the allocation of capital. You have to know your alternatives and be prepared to adapt as things occur. And a key to our business is having the ability to say no. We reject 99 out of 100 investment opportunities."

Bill began his career by analyzing his professional alternatives.

"Even in my mid-twenties I was still experimenting and exploring—theater, bartending, driving a truck—I sought things outside the box of a middle-class upbringing in Indianapolis," Bill said. "It is valuable to not try to progress through life in a linear fashion. Those experiences made me better at what I do today."

Then, once he settled on a career in the investment field, Bill studied his alternatives again within the trade.

"At Continental Bank, my first job was in multinational lending where we serviced companies like IBM and GE," he said. "I was talking to assistant treasurers about derivatives instead of dealing with people and products. I asked to go to the bank's Midwest division because I wanted to work with entrepreneurs, with people who were making things and building organizations. My alternative—more esoteric finance—provided good training and background, but I preferred a more tangible line of work. I decided when I was thirty that I wanted to run something and build businesses and took a series of jobs that I thought would prepare me for that."

Bill has looked to role models and books throughout his career for alternative ways to think, lead, and do deals. Biographies especially give him precedents for how different approaches to life, leadership, and business can yield different outcomes.

In an obsolete software planner called Sidekick, Bill keeps a category called "the well-furnished mind." It is his book list, and topics of the books range from economics and fiction to philosophy and history. He reads for two hours every day and always travels with a book in his briefcase. For Bill, honing his imagination and instincts are important for forecasting outcomes.

"The intellectual exploration that comes through reading is a big part of preparation," he explained. "I believe I am better able to analyze and implement a business decision because I have studied how Reagan led by focusing on a few big principles or how Lincoln did the same thing during the Civil War."

Allied offers financing at all levels of a company's capital structure, from senior or subordinate debt to equity. Allied tries to distinguish itself as an alternative to the multitude of private equity firms by emphasizing long-term partnerships with its portfolio companies.

During any given year, Bill and his team come across thousands of opportunities for investment. These alternatives are informed by numerous ways to structure the deals—for example, various combinations of debt and equity, decisions about minority versus control positions, whether or not to ask for board representation—which can lead to different relationships between Allied and these companies. Bill and his team have to think through myriad risk/return alternatives to determine the correct strategy for each investment.

They narrow the list down in part by looking for businesses that seem to offer the potential for long-term growth. "Does the company generate free cash flow, high return on capital, and has it been doing so consistently for years?" Bill said as he lists Allied's criteria for determining if a business is a viable investment alternative. "And if so, why? You often find a good business at the wrong price, or a good business at a decent price but with poor management," Bill explained. "You need to be able to check the business against your criteria, and walking away is always an alternative. Then you can stay in touch and the deal may come back years later."

Two other critical factors in Allied's forecasting of outcomes are the leadership of a business and how a company could relate to others in Allied's portfolio.

One company in the portfolio as of 2006, Advantage Sales and Marketing, is the result of a merger of sixteen consumer packaged goods brokers nationwide.

"Talk about herding cats," Bill said. "There were sixteen companies headed by sixteen very different, yet successful entrepreneurs. For our deal team it was essential to assess the best leader and the right leadership group overall. You go into meetings and especially look for how leaders treat others; who doesn't talk when others are talking; whether a CEO is talking all about himself or herself or is focused on a vision for the company. People reveal themselves pretty readily in the first thirty to sixty minutes. We're looking for ethical, smart and industry-savvy leaders."

Portfolio fit means evaluating how Allied can leverage the skill sets, products, and location of a potential investment. "We ask ourselves," said Walton, "'What we can bring to the table to help a particular business grow and what might it bring to other companies already in our portfolio?' Our core competencies are with business and consumer services and consumer products companies."

Bill continued, "We are laying bricks one on top of the other to some degree. The idea is to invest or lend to companies that interrelate. One company might provide financing or merger and acquisition advice; two companies might help each other with supply chain consulting or even import assistance. For example, one of our companies with offices in Shanghai helps source product from China for several other portfolio companies."

Bill also recognizes that potential companies for his portfolio also have alternatives to Allied that they consider.

"You analyze their alternatives as part of any deal," he said. "We know our competitors, and we try to make clear to potential partners that we think we have distinctive competitive advantage as a highly transparent company with permanent capital and a long list of partners to share their experience."

Allied's final factor in evaluating alternatives is to analyze how an investment contributes to an unabashedly optimistic vision of capitalism. While not the primary factor in making investment decisions, the contribution of a company to economic improvement for employees, consumers, and communities factors distinctly into the decision.

"It is a proof of our analysis that most of the companies in Allied's portfolio are providing interesting goods and services that contribute to the social good in and of itself," Bill said. "Our companies are led by people of integrity and when we wind up making money, it is based on real production and creation. We've created a lot of jobs, helped a lot of local economies, and created a lot of wealth. Preparation for an investment has to factor this sort of thing in."

We all are regularly faced with investment decisions—of our time, energy, and capital. Bill's story reminds us that assembling and evaluating alternative outcomes and pulling back to study the larger landscape help make the investment productive in the long term.

ALTERNATIVE TASTES

Robert Parker

If you want to know how to analyze alternatives in both careers and wines, feel free to invite Robert Parker, publisher of *The Wine Advocate,* to your home for dinner. He loves a party, and he will come prepared. You may panic about selecting red or white, Bordeaux or Napa, Rothschild or Coppola. Don't worry. Bob always brings the wine.

I, like many of my friends, used to find the world of wine daunting. So many brands, so many price points, so much elitism. Then I started to read Bob's wine criticism, and I felt as if the crisp Anglo-Saxon language of Hemingway had replaced the impenetrable linguistic concoctions of James Joyce. I could understand Bob's writing; I tended to agree with his judgments; and, most of all, I learned about wine and geography and history while I simultaneously pleased my palate.

Bob Parker has democratized wine, but he has not sullied it as a commodity. He is no Hollywood studio or fast-food chain threatening the sacrosanctity of French cinema or cuisine. In fact, Bob is more of a celebrity in France than in the United States. He received the Legion of Honor medal from former president Jacques Chirac. He gets recognized in trains and restaurants throughout Europe. He is the son of a dairy farmer who followed his passion and prepares like a virtuoso surgeon.

And a key to Bob's success is his ability to analyze alternatives. He focuses on two critical decisions: in the long term, his alternative ways to approach his role as a critic; more immediately, the selection and ranking of alternative wines.

I'm going to look at each of these. I hope you will see that there is little difference between Bob analyzing his alternatives in his business and you in yours.

"I am not some extraordinary wine talent," Bob said during an interview at his home in the Maryland horse country. "I just work harder, prepare more, than most people in this line of work. That preparation consumes me. It is what I live for. It reminds me of the time when the talk-show host Charlie Rose asked me how I got good at what I do. I said I just prepare more. Charlie said Michael Jordan told him the same thing. I just practice harder."

While his bulldog snored beside me on the sofa, Bob was much more interested in talking about his preparation method than about his accolades or adventures.

As a critic, Bob has undoubtedly transformed the wine industry. He has made enemies of some of the most powerful vineyards in the world by criticizing vintages that other critics regularly hailed. He has given new prominence to unheralded vineyards. Along the way he has brought objectivity and credibility to the field of wine criticism.

To do this, Bob very early on analyzed the ethical alternatives that a critic faces. Far worse than the film or art world, wine critics cherished their incestuous relationship with the wine industry. Free wine and luxurious lodging were the perks for lazy and compromised critics for years.

Bob saw this alternative and determined that another route was more appealing to him and better for the industry. He insisted on absolute independence from wine châteaus; his brand has been built as much on that credibility as on his talent or prose.

"I even buy my wines to taste," Bob said. "It's the only way to be certain that you are not being handed an unrepresentative sample of that vintage. I want to taste the wine that my readers taste."

In determining his approach to his career, Bob applies his legal training to his role as a critic. Rather than the effete artistry to which many critics aspire, he prefers the alternative of treating a critique of a wine as he would the construction of a legal case. Bob practiced law for a few years, but grew tired of the competition and repetitiveness of his work in the farm credit banks. But he stays devoted to the method that solid legal training fosters.

"I think that one of the things that was revolutionary when I started was my work ethic," Bob said. "That came from a good law school training. I transferred the whole process of building a case to my work in wine. The methodical nature of the law influenced how I approached my criticism. You have to master the facts and precedents to understand your case."

Bob used an alternative approach to answer the main charge against any sort of critic: that it is easy to criticize it but hard to do it. Bob bought a vineyard. He practices what he preaches.

"Critics are like eunuchs—you talk a lot about it but you can't do it," Bob said. "I identified that weakness not so much to build a stronger reputation but simply to become a more informed critic. Going through all these decisions in managing a vineyard has definitely made me a better critic. And it gives me a newfound respect for the people who make wine for a living. When I go into a winery or estate, I see it as a privilege that they are allowing me there. I may not like their wine, but I want to be as professional as possible. My own work on my vineyard in Oregon has taught me that to visit is a privilege and not some critic's right."

Of course, Bob methodically analyzes alternatives when

he judges the wine itself. He has established a simple but comprehensive set of criteria for ranking the alternative wines that he analyzes. The outcome is a clear and accessible guide to quality wines at all price levels from innumerable regions. He can't shake his legal training; logic and well-structured arguments make Bob reader-friendly.

An insight into his approach comes from his own little wine tasting club near his home. Most people bring a wide range of wines when it is their turn to host the tasting. Bob always brings wines from the same vintage. He believes that you can only truly compare wines of the same peer group. The rest, though fun, is unscientific.

Bob limits his criteria when tasting a wine to three. Does it look healthy? How does it smell? And what are its discernible components in your mouth? This very specific focus helps Bob be certain that his ultimate critique is consistent. His alternative outcomes fit into categories that his readers have grown familiar with.

In terms of appearance, Bob can determine a wine's texture and body and keeps diligent notes that allow him to compare it to its peers. He chooses to emphasize a wine's visual beauty as part of his criticism.

"You see it before you taste it," Bob said. "You can never forget that. The colors—some of them are so intense and extraordinary that it inevitably becomes a critical component."

Similarly, you usually smell a wine before you taste it, and in Bob's criticism smell and taste blend into a sixth sense.

"I try not to get carried away with metaphor," Bob said. "But the smell of a wine is an important alternative in judging it. Pleasing or not, good or bad or neutral. You shouldn't get carried away but the categories of quality are undeniable."

Bob tries to keep his analysis of taste as uncomplicated as his sense of smell.

"Here you are really looking for a harmony among the different components of the taste," Bob explained. "I'm going to note a floral taste but I'm not going to get carried away and say lilac. It's like a work of art. If something is out of balance or proportion in a painting, you notice it. I'm looking for that balance of all the instruments in the piece. There are so many alternatives when you are judging a wine, so many possible criteria. I try to determine the benchmark wines in a genre and simply use them as the standards."

Bob also had to choose among alternate ways to write about his experiences with wine. Putting criticism to paper is as important in Bob's field as all the preparation for tasting and judging. Wine writing before Bob, and much of it still, spills over with pedantry and hyperbole. Bob looks for the same thing in his writing as he does in a good wine: balance.

"A former head of Christie's wine auctions once said a certain wine tasted 'like an old dowager with her makeup cracking amidst her wrinkles,' or something like that," Bob remarked. "Of the same wine, I simply said it tastes like vinegar. I try to keep it simple for my readers."

Bob's face lights up when he says that the purpose of a good wine is to trigger that slight sense of euphoria at a meal with good friends. I cheer up a bit, too, when I think of how Bob prepared for his shift from lawyer to critic and how he prepares for the daily tasks he faces in judging so many wines. The judicious analysis of alternative outcomes according to refined criteria helped prepare Bob to become the international standard for judging wine.

KEY POINTS

ALTERNATIVES

- There are usually multiple outcomes to a task that satisfy your objectives to varying degrees. So it is important to forecast alternative outcomes in a methodical way—for better or for worse, you have to try to foresee just what you may be getting yourself into.

- Forecasting your potential results helps you shape your strategy by adding or subtracting steps that may guide you more toward one outcome or another.

- The use of this principle at this stage keeps you focused on the linkage between the means and the end— between your preparation and its results.

- The success of Taylor Branch's history of the Civil Rights movement in America is in large part due to the methodical approach he took when analyzing the alternative ways to research history, do interviews, and establish a narrative voice.

- Bill Walton habitually weighs the alternative outcomes— be it for a sentence he is formulating or a deal he is making. His forecasting leads to long-term investments that are consistent with the goals and portfolio of Allied Capital.

- In the wine world of Bob Parker, there are alternative wines to judge and alternative ways to judge them. Bob's determination that he wanted a clear, accessible, and independent outcome in his wine criticism helped him transform an industry.

6

IT'S IN YOUR BEST INTEREST TO KNOW THEIR INTERESTS

Define the Interests

We tend to get stuck in the trap of thinking that only speakers, entertainers, and athletes have audiences. In fact, everyone has an audience. The audience begins with yourself and those for whom you work and ends with the client or group in front of you. Making sure you understand who your audience is and what really motivates them is critical to successful preparation.

When it comes to understanding their interests, you may be required to probe past the obvious. Probing, or questioning a client or counterpart in a methodical way to obtain relevant information, is a way that supports preparation. It can give you information to determine a point of view, develop potential leverage, or uncover hidden, unstated, or unknown needs or objectives.

Just as you determine your objectives at the outset of preparation, so, too, should you determine the interests of your client, audience, or counterpart.

For example, your boss may assign you a project, but he or she may place even more emphasis on the next project that the current project triggers. You can probably only determine this by probing your boss—questioning his or her interests in the result.

The buyers of your products may want to satisfy a specific need which the product fulfills or may want simply to be associated with your brand and get access to other product lines that you sell. You can only determine this by probing them for their needs and objectives.

Buying or selling a home is an emotional event and some people take parts of the process very personally. As a buyer or seller who wants the best price but who also wants to maintain a certain level of professionalism and emotional calm, it is in your best interest to examine the interests of the other party. By probing them, you can identify their emotional flashpoints and underlying needs such as a quick closing or a certain move-in schedule. A seller may set a high price for her home, but her primary interest may be moving to Florida in two months. You may discover that after politely but thoroughly probing her needs and her statements.

You can reduce anxiety when you know its source or

cause. Identifying the true interests of angry or agitated clients can help you address their most pressing needs and thereby reduce the anxiety on both sides. Knowledge of their interests can help you focus on your objectives while not letting their emotions distract you from your goal.

To define their interests, you have to be interested in them. You treat your client or counterpart as a topic that merits your attention. Most of them—whether boring or angry, aggressive or taciturn, sharp or plodding—have a set of interests that you want to understand, not only to help yourself prepare but also because they are interesting in and of themselves.

THE BRASS OR THE BUCKS

In most challenges I face, I look at what the parties are really after.

Probing served me well when I was representing the concertmaster of a major symphony. He wanted a raise of $40 a week or else he "wanted out" as he told me in an emotional outburst. $40 per week—and "they" wouldn't give it to him! He was already earning almost $200,000 per year, so why was another $2,000 so important to him? What was his real interest?

Probing not only makes you a better negotiator, it makes you a better representative of your client. By probing, I learned that this small raise would mean the symphony was paying the concertmaster double scale, making him the only member to receive that level of pay. His real interest, then, was not money but status. Or, better said, the status associated with a certain financial standing.

However, as I stated at the outset, you need to probe both sides—yourself (understanding your objectives) and the other guy. I probed to understand his objectives. But it turns out that the symphony had some significant interests here, too. The orchestra could not satisfy his request because its collective bargaining agreement with the players provided that if anyone achieved double scale, then everyone would be eligible and other raises would be triggered. This would bust the symphony's budget. So my objective became reconciling my client's interests with those of the symphony. What could be affordable signifiers of status that the symphony could grant to a world-class musician without breaking the bank? Without throwing their whole financial structure out of whack?

Well, quite simply, we started with a brass nameplate. Only the conductor had one on the door of his dressing room, and now the concertmaster would have one, too. My client loved this badge of status.

Then, more significantly, we got the symphony to grant the concertmaster first-class travel on all international tours. He would be flying with the major donors and conductor, eating the same fine food and drinking the same fine wine at the front of the plane. He was satisfied with the status of his seat.

And because we discovered that they could get the upgrades through barter with the airline, the symphony was satisfied, too. They spent $39.95 on the brass plate and nothing on the upgrades. He let go of his demand for $40 a week.

A MEMORIAL FULL OF INTERESTS

Holocaust memorials, like many memorials, seem to invite conflict. Family, pain, and commemoration combine to make a perfect battleground for divergent and emotional interests.

I led a committee charged with overseeing the creation of a Holocaust memorial in the city of Baltimore. I have probably been involved in thousands of business deals and civic endeavors, but I have never experienced a project in which it was so critical to define each constituent's interests as part of the preparation process. The higher the level of emotion, the more important it is to probe the interests of all sides. Without embracing this preparation principle, I am convinced that we would have been left with a memorial as much to internal strife as to our ancestors and all those who suffered.

As many know, designing a building or monument brings the designer in all of us out of the closet. How to put sentiment and suffering into a physical structure? Impossible, I would say. But we had to come up with a design, and better minds than mine articulated and built a physical representation that satisfied the emotional longing of many of Baltimore's citizens. We appeased the amateur designers around town by including them in a series of presentations and discussions. We identified their interest—to feel that they had contributed to the spirit of the design—and addressed it.

But the bigger question became the issue of what was going to be inscribed on the monument. Would it be a universal message and commemoration or one specific to the loss of life by only Jews in the Holocaust? Would the memorial acknowledge non-Jews who perished?

In meetings boiling with emotion, there were survivors who would stand up in our meetings and roll up their sleeves and show the numbers on their arms. They urged us not to reach beyond the specificity and horror of what they went through. Others, both citizens and community relations experts and advocates, urged that the memorial address all those who died in the Holocaust.

Ultimately we recognized in the inscription the six million Jews who perished but also the non-Jews who suffered or died while seeking to offer them assistance. I still cherish a letter from Dr. Louis Kaplan, a great educator and religious leader, acknowledging work I did in getting at the interest of Holocaust survivors while acknowledging the sacrifice and pain of others. We could only balance interests by first identifying them and clearly stating them.

The meetings that led up to the compromise were so fraught with emotion that I would go home with my shirt soaked with sweat. I was trying to hold these two factions together and get at their interests. By probing and letting them speak, by reformulating their own thoughts for them and helping everyone realize how closely all the interests were aligned, we minimized internal conflict and achieved our larger goal of memorializing both the specific and universal tragedy of the Holocaust.

SAVING EVERYONE TIME AND MONEY

It is hard to believe, but the definition of the financial instruments called "securities" under the securities laws in the 1970s still lacked clarity. I was the new securities commissioner for the State of Maryland, and we were dealing with efforts by regulators to define the instruments so that states could better regulate their offer and sale. In our state, my office understood the definition to be something like this: securities are contracts in which one party invests money in the expectation of a return that will be won solely through the efforts of others. That is, the investor puts up the funds but has no role in the potential use and growth of those funds. The investor relies on the work of others to generate the return.

Early during my tenure, I was alerted to a group of businessmen engaged in real estate transactions that "smelled" like securities. They promised returns to buyers beyond the normal market amount. Their offer and sale of beach condominium properties included the promise of significant returns through their renting the units to third parties to produce these returns to investors. My view was that they were engaged in more than typical real estate transactions—they were offering and selling securities or "investment contracts." And they were not providing the appropriate disclosure required of investments under the securities law. In an age when courts had still not defined securities clearly enough, my sense was that these transactions constituted the sale of securities without the required registration and disclosure. Their business was growing, and a legal case was looming.

Before acting rashly, however, my office acknowledged the murkiness of the law at that time and decided to probe the interests of this company to see if we could find a route to a nonjudicial settlement. Were they aware of their potential violations? Were they taking advantage of the law? Of the cloudiness of the law? Or might they simply be oblivious to the implications of their transactions given the evolving state of securities law? Should I fine them or seek a stronger punishment like jail? Or merely seek to correct their procedures and set right their past errors?

By probing them and their customers, we determined that they were not bad guys, and that they honestly believed that they were engaged in the sale of real estate and not securities. They truly did not foresee the need for registration under securities law. They were perfectly willing to comply with the law and even offered to undo the transactions. So we were able to easily work out a settlement in which the company did not admit or deny wrongdoing but did agree to comply with registration going forward and offer rescission retroactively.

This is another example of how defining the interests can save you time and money. I was not looking forward to a protracted court fight; time and efficiency were critically important to me because we were such a small and young office; and the law itself needed further clarification before I could start to carry a big stick.

In the next three profiles, Ambassador Charlene Barshefsky shows how to gain the confidence of counterparts by understanding their interests. Scott Pilarz, S.J., the president of the University of Scranton, and John Dionne of the Blackstone Group determine the motivations of their audience to win their support for a cause. And broadcaster Bob Costas illustrates how to connect with an audience regardless of its size.

THE AMBASSADOR OF INTERESTS

Charlene Barshefsky

Charlene Barshefsky does much of her preparation by defining the interests of parties she is dealing with in high-level international negotiations. Yet her relentless pursuit of an understanding of those interests is applicable to your negotiations with people in almost any context.

The first words out of Charlene's mouth, after an exchange of pleasantries, are: "I can't separate preparation from who I am. It is who I am." Talk about a sense of identity.

Charlene Barshefsky is senior international partner at Wilmer Hale LLP, a law firm in Washington, D.C. She was the U.S. trade representative with the rank of ambassador from 1997 to 2001. One of the highlights of her career is the heralded trade agreement that brought the Chinese into the World Trade Organization.

Trade is a lightning rod topic, and Charlene held a lighting rod job—perhaps one of the most thankless jobs in Washington. To survive and to succeed she relied on methodical preparation. And of the preparation principles, she exhibits an extraordinary ability to study and define the interests of a counterpart, client, or audience.

The counterparts Charlene faced were the tough customers of international trade and negotiations—especially the Japanese, Chinese, and Brazilian negotiators. In particular, the Chinese have a reputation for being stony-faced and making demands that show little room for compromise. As the ascendant economic power on the planet, they start from the premise that they have more leverage than any other party at the table.

The Chinese negotiations began early on with the controversial topic of intellectual property rights. Charlene, as she always does, prepared by first researching as extensively as possible the backgrounds and interests of every member of the Chinese negotiating team. She focused on a member of the State Council (the equivalent of our U.S. cabinet) whose scientific background was extensive. Charlene gained at least an amateur's mastery of this negotiator's field and research achievements. She queried him about his research. They developed a strong working relationship because he sensed her genuine interest in his career and intellectual calling.

"He was impressed that I could discuss his field even in the most general of terms," Charlene said. "I prepare by reading widely. And almost any topic interests me intellectually. In fact, I almost prefer to read outside of my field and even outside of history and politics. So I really looked at this interaction as a chance to both develop a negotiating rapport and also satisfy my own intellectual curiosity. And I think he sensed my genuine interest in his work."

Because the early negotiations with the Chinese were centered on the controversial issue of intellectual property protection, Charlene made sure to appeal to the scientist's background. Her definition of his interests became a critical factor in the success of the negotiation.

"I linked our efforts to better protect intellectual property to his own recognition that scientific investigation also involves a proprietary component," Charlene explained. "Any scientist or researcher anywhere takes pride in their findings and probably feels some sort of ownership of that discovery or finding. So this member of the State Council, with his strong scientific background, became very helpful in articulating to Chinese decision makers the importance of the issue."

This is an example of how Charlene identified the interests of her counterparts on a one-on-one level. She applied the principle with equal conviction and success on the national level, too. Prior to the negotiations with the Chinese, she tried to gain as wide a mastery of Chinese history, politics, and economics as possible.

China had been in negotiations to get into the WTO for many years. And the nation's argument for accession was not always sufficiently based on the merits. They exhibited a sense of entitlement based on size, growth, and the hype that accompanies the Chinese economy today.

"It was pretty clear that China thought they would accede on a political basis," Barshefsky noted. "This is not the way it works. So I had to help them understand what accession meant, but explain it to them in a way that addressed other interests that the Chinese may not even have fully recognized. So we put together what I called the roadmap—an eight- or nine-page internal document, which outlined in general terms what areas of the economy would be covered and what had to be encompassed. They did not realize that this meant every good that they made; agriculture; their service sectors; tax policies; electricity, water, and gas; automobiles; tariff rates; the banking sector and branch banking; the telecom sector—the list applied to everything tradable, as well as to intellectual property rights."

So for Charlene and her team, the challenge became aligning the economic interests of the Chinese with their political ambitions.

Charlene realized that the Chinese are incredibly pragmatic when it comes to their economic reforms. So she played to their economic interests rather than their national political ego.

"I tried to reconfigure a lot of what we were asking for in the talks in a way that dovetailed with their internal reform program," she said. "I also focused my efforts on the most farsighted person on their team. I knew he realized what I was doing, but he became the perfect internal partner to help change the Chinese mind-set."

Charlene had delved so deeply that she knew the interests of the Chinese perhaps even better than they knew their own. So focused on their stature in Asia and their accession into the big leagues of the international community, the Chinese were emphasizing a superficial interest over a more profound and long-term one: the complete and successful reform of their economy. Recognition was one thing, but success in the economic arena would bring far more substantial benefits than any designation as part of the WTO. Playing to their interests by reminding them of their higher objective, Charlene and her team subtly changed the whole approach of the Chinese.

I often see this in business dealings or negotiations: because you have a different perspective, you can actually bring your client, counterpart, or audience to reprioritize their interests or even identify a new or higher interest. This can only occur through preparation—through spending time analyzing their interests. Charlene was able to bring the Chinese to recognize their critical economic interests and the way participation in the WTO would help further them. Her way of probing their needs, concerns, and ambitions is an example for anyone engaged in negotiating an agreement, selling a product, or presenting an idea.

PLAYING TO THEIR INTERESTS

John Dionne/Scott Pilarz

One is a brash Wall Street financier. The other is a studious university president and Jesuit priest. Together, they raise funds for the school they love by learning the interests of their donors. And they serve as an example for any of us seeking to have other people buy into our ideas or products.

On the face of it, John Dionne and Scott Pilarz make for a pretty good version of the odd couple. John is a senior managing director at the private equity Blackstone Group and chairman of the board at the University of Scranton; Scott is a Jesuit priest and Scranton's president. John is an accountant by training; Scott is an expert in obscure English poetry.

But scratch beneath the surface a bit and you see why the two may be the perfect pair of preparers to bring the scrappy University of Scranton onto a bigger stage in American higher education.

Both grew up watching fathers who worked like dogs to get their sons educated at Jesuit universities—John at Scranton and Scott at Georgetown. Both hold a commitment to service and to the moral as well as intellectual obligations of colleges. Both drink Scotch. And both prepare incessantly for their challenge of raising $100 million for Scranton's capital campaign.

Scranton does not have as many wealthy alums as most schools of its caliber in this country. When Scranton first decided to undertake a capital campaign, it hired a well-known consultant to determine its feasibility. This is typical. The feedback was poor: the resources weren't there among alums to realize a campaign amount worth announcing. So Scott and John fired that consultant and hired another who came back with only slightly better news.

John and Scott then realized they needed to make a total commitment to defining the interests of their donors in order to achieve a target that far surpassed anything either consultant would consider feasible.

Whether they are shooting for an eight-figure gift from the head of a huge insurance company or a smattering of five-figure gifts from working-class alums up and down the East Coast, they apply a checklist of items that they use to attempt to ascertain the interests of givers.

"We realize we have to know these people very well," John said in an interview at his firm's Park Avenue office. "We have to know them inside out in a way few schools do. I don't think many schools try to get to know the interests of their donors as much as we do. First, it's a basic courtesy. But you really have to look at this as their giving a check and wanting to see results. And because we need the money more than most schools, we need to get it right. So, yes, knowing their interests and being committed to satisfying them is what this is all about."

The University of Scranton sits in the middle of a former coal town. The popular television program *The Office* is set in Scranton, but the college has developed a buzz among graduating high schoolers across the country more for being a student-friendly place—close to New York but far enough away to be affordable, and small enough to offer access to professors.

Enrollment has doubled to four thousand, and you are almost as likely now to meet students from California and Florida as from Pennsylvania and New Jersey.

Yet the infrastructure has not been updated in fifty years. Cozy has become cramped; quaint is now antiquated. And Scranton, as a Jesuit school whose operations were to a large degree funded by the Jesuit order, never focused on its endowment like many other schools in America.

You get the sense today that universities treat endowments like hedge funds treat fees: big for the sake of status. The *U.S. News and World Report* rankings that emphasize endowments no doubt play a big factor.

So John and Scott are starting from behind, with the stakes all the higher for it.

"At most we get one hour of real time with donors," Scott said. "So the question becomes what part of the Scranton story can I tell effectively in one hour? What part of this great story do they want to hear?"

To prepare to define these interests, John and Scott have developed a preparation method that they use for almost every presentation, meal, or cocktail chat.

They have what they call a "SWAT team" that studies the potential donor's background and then gives a report that assesses both the person's interests as a student at Scranton and possible new interests now. Then John and Scott run through their checklist before scripting their encounter.

The first part of the checklist deals with the past. What

affinities can they latch onto in their pitch? Was the potential donor active in sports? Theater? Science?

"Some of the work really is historical research," Scott said. "What were they involved with during their student days? Does that interest fit our current needs? This works well with the new campus center and more space for student activities."

And then they choreograph their probing. Scott and John know who will ask what questions to dig deeper into the potential donor's interests, convictions, and vision for his or her alma mater. As a result of defining the interests, they are able to better shape their pitch.

For example, Scott acknowledges that Scranton is a bit behind the curve in terms of lobbying potential donors who might best be described as "athletic alumni." This is becoming a critical part of their campaign efforts, though sports teams at Scranton only now are achieving the prominence that they have long held at most American schools. Scranton kids were for the most part commuters who were working jobs after classes.

Then there is the appeal to nostalgia. That is an interest that most of us harbor for a place where we spent four years of our youth.

"Some alums are simply nostalgic, and we try to indulge that," Scott said. "For instance, we use the university archives of photographs to celebrate the rich history here. People like to be reminded of how far we have come. And there is a lot of romance about educating coal miners and their kids."

The universal appeal of the coal mining history also is a specific part of the Scranton brand that Scott and John do not underestimate.

"We are defined by our history as a coal town," Scott said. "So, particularly for older alums, we have to appeal to their interest in that self-definition."

As for contemporary interests, John and Scott identify interests in religion, social service, and, for lack of a better word, bang-for-your-buck economics.

More conservative Catholics tend to gravitate toward campus ministry. More liberal Catholics will usually be interested in giving to international and domestic service projects.

"Nursing education is also a popular cause these days, since people are aware of a nursing shortage," Scott said. "We can make a compelling case for science, too. Americans are falling woefully behind in science education, and that resonates with a lot of potential donors."

Finally, the bang-for-the-buck interest of some donors—and one that especially appeals to the banker in John—is analyzed.

"We make the case that we are doing very special things on a shoestring here," John said. "You can give a few thousand or even a few million dollars to a school with a large endowment and it's impossible to trace the effect you have. Here we sell to donors that we are giving them a better bang for their buck. We try to make as clear as possible the effect that each dollar has. Trace it for them. That can have an amazing effect that almost rivals seeing your name on a building."

John even decided to prepare for the campaign by reaching beyond what he calls the "sugar bowl" of Scranton alums. He tapped into a group of New York businessmen who appreciate his bang-for-the-buck philosophy and love an underdog story. He brings up a student every year to meet them who represents the kind of student that he and Scott want Scranton to produce.

The underdog university from coal country will someday have a bunch of new buildings and much firmer financial footing because of the methodical definition of interests. And the odd couple who spend so much time defining the interests of donors offers anyone who is asking for something a lesson in how to prepare to ask for it.

AN INTERESTED AUDIENCE

Bob Costas

Bob Costas's presentations are normally made to millions of viewers. But whether you make a presentation to colleagues in a conference room or to the world on the airwaves, the impact you have is determined by interests you define.

Say you watch a game with a momentous, even historic ending. The Miracle on Ice at the Olympics in 1980; the Game 7 World Series defeat in 2001 of the Yankees by the Arizona Diamondbacks; Joe Montana's pass to Dwight Clark to beat the Dallas Cowboys in the playoffs in 1982. There is likely to be one major difference between the way you and Bob Costas take in the moment.

You or I would remember the play; Bob will remember the way the play was called. Bob sees the drama and craft on the field or floor, but even more he sees the artistry in the announcer who narrates the story. And then he ponders the preparation that went into that narrative moment in the same way you or I would inevitably turn our thoughts from the play itself to how the team pulled the play off.

Why? Bob strives to see almost every sporting event through both the eyes and the ears of its audience rather than its actors. It is not about his interests, but yours. That is an old-school concept, but he realizes that the call and explanation of the play subconsciously form a big part of the viewer's pleasure.

THE CRAFT OF DEFINING INTERESTS

Craftsmanship in broadcasting is giving way to bombast. So what is so striking about listening to Bob Costas talk about it is the way he refers to it as a craft and how he equates craftsmanship with preparation.

In the hyperhip restaurant of New York's Hudson Hotel one day, Bob does not so much turn heads as ears. The people seated around us are craning their necks to listen to Bob talk about his role models, preparation, and audience.

Preparation in broadcasting is in large part about fulfilling the interests of the audience. That recognition, combined with the preparation that leads to the marriage of delivery and content, makes for maestros like Bob.

Master preparers almost always look at the way mentors or role models prepare. In Bob's case, he still studies predecessors and colleagues for three qualities: their ability to capture and enhance the drama at hand; their nuanced way of relating detail and facts; and their general tone (including humor) and integrity. He uses precedents to approach the definition of his audience's interests.

For drama, Bob points to Al Michaels's famous narration of the defeat of the then Soviet Union by the ragtag American Olympic hockey team in 1980. Michaels may or may not have had that line—"Do you believe in miracles?"—prepared prior to the end of the game. But, given the political tenor of the country at the time and the snowballing interest in the team, it was an exemplary combination of concise delivery and authentic emotion that enhanced his audience's viewing experience. He addressed their interests.

Bob cites many broadcasts by ABC's Jim McKay, but especially his coverage of the murder of the Israeli athletes at the 1972 Munich Olympics.

"A remarkable blend of professional skill and personal empathy," Bob said. "He didn't just report the story. He *felt* it, and the audience felt it along with him. Since the event was unexpected and unpredictable, no specific preparation was possible. Jim's preparation was his whole career as a writer and broadcaster, combined with the experience and perspective of a mature and thoughtful man, who had led an interesting and varied life. He brought all that to bear in those moments."

As an example of effective delivery of detail, Bob points to Tom Hammond, his colleague at NBC. You may have watched the Preakness Stakes in 2006 when the great horse and Triple Crown hopeful Barbaro damaged his leg coming out of the gate. Hammond has a degree in equine science and lives in Lexington, Kentucky, spending a good portion of his life around racehorses and racing people. That preparation helped Hammond to both inform and console the audience while reporting on Barbaro's condition immediately after the horse's fall.

"Hammond wove details about equine science with a great sense of the drama of what had just happened," Bob said. "He gave the audience what they wanted in terms of both information and drama. I watch moments like that and keep learning. I use them as examples for how to prepare myself."

As for personal presentation, Bob finds Los Angeles Dodgers broadcaster Vin Scully's dedication to his craft just as impressive as his eloquence and one-of-a-kind voice. "Here's a guy who has been at it for nearly sixty years and received every possible accolade and award. Yet he never rests on his laurels. He prepares for a ho-hum Wednesday game in August just as if it were a playoff game. He respects his audience, his craft, and his own reputation too much to do otherwise. The best announcers always respect their audience; so, in a sense you prepare just by observing professionals like them."

THE INTERESTS OF BOB'S VARIED AUDIENCES

Translating these examples into his own career, Bob points to three situations in which preparation produced results he hopes satisfied the interests of his audience.

In terms of narrating the dramatic moment, Bob holds up his description of Michael Jordan's last shot before retiring as a Chicago Bull in the NBA Championship Game in 1998. Obviously, announcers cannot work from a script. But good ones like Bob nevertheless do anticipate scenarios.

In this case, the world was wondering if Jordan would retire after the season. No one knew, but Bob was focused on the fact that that lack of certainty made the drama of the last shot even greater. So as Jordan let the ball soar and paused like a statue with his hand in the air to admire the ball's trajectory, Bob was ready.

After calling the play, and resetting the score and time remaining, Bob offered these comments over a series of slow-motion replays: "If that's the final chapter, what a way to close the book!"

The best narrations complement or enhance the drama. And Bob did it that night by drawing on the interest of his audience in the possibility that this might be the last time we would watch the magnificent Jordan.

In terms of balancing detail with that drama, Bob faces this challenge for weeks at a time as he hosts the world from NBC's Olympic studio. No audience wants too much detail, nor do they want a drumming up of drama. And yet, given the number of hours that Bob has to fill during the Olympics, either extreme can be tempting.

"My preparation for the massiveness of the event includes keeping myself from overpreparing," Bob said. "It would be easy to fall into the trap of trying to fit in every detail about the host location, the particulars of a less prominent competition, and the great human interest stories of so many athletes, but you don't want to wear the audience out. You are likely to use only about 10 to 20 percent of what you prepare. You just don't know exactly which 20 percent. You have to adapt as things unfold and have the restraint not to force in information that, no matter how interesting, may not fit the tone, pace, and circumstances of the broadcast. The host's job is to be a good generalist and provide an overview. Most of the particulars should come from the experts at the event venues. I find that approach probably best serves the audience's interests."

There is one more exemplary situation I want to cover here—Bob's approach to interviews.

Most of our careers are undoubtedly filled more with one-on-one interactions—phone calls and face-to-face meetings with the boss—than with presentations or public speaking. In those scenarios, a good strategy is to try to become an interviewer.

Bob is a top-notch interviewer. Of course, it is easy enough to distinguish himself, given the trend toward fawning blather in television interviews today. But Bob prepares for his interviews in a way few broadcasters do today—he visualizes himself in the position of his audience. Bob realizes that his audience likely already knows the story of the person he is speaking with. So he searches for the new angle, the new anecdote, or the twist on the old story that will interest his audience anew.

"You can't let your preparation for an interview interfere with your listening," Bob said. "You can't let preparation control you. But at the same time you are usually dealing with people who have been interviewed a lot. They are naturally interested in a new question or a new insight, in something different. So you almost want them to say 'how did you know that?' I was interviewing the film director Barry Levinson once and found out that in an early job he once edited B-movies for a local television station. He was so delighted to tell the story that it led him to open up on other things, and everything just flowed from there."

All of these ways of defining and fulfilling the interests of the audience are as applicable in other trades as they are in broadcasting. Bob makes a fundamental commitment to defining the interest of his audience: he listens, probes, and scripts. His preparation template serves as an example for all of us who have to engage other people as part of our living.

KEY POINTS

INTERESTS

- Preparation is not an egocentric activity that you perform in a vacuum. You prepare yourself for your audience—your clients, colleagues, customers, or counterparts.
- Applying the principles to your audience helps you define their interests and also know their objectives, precedents, alternative outcomes, and team.
- Probing is a key tool for knowing their interests—you probe them directly with questions, research their histories, and also seek information from people who have worked with them or against them.
- A master negotiator, Charlene Barshefsky studies the interests of her counterparts in such detail that she often helps them clarify their own objectives. She also looks for the ways in which their personal interests may overlap with the issue at hand and tries to link the two together in her presentations.
- Fund-raising requires a thorough identification of a donor's interests. Scott Pilarz, S.J., and John Dionne tailor their pitches to the interests that their methodical probing and research uncovers.
- Bob Costas has an audience of millions, but the way he studies his viewers' expectations applies to any field. From his subject matter to his delivery, Bob knows that an understanding of what the audience wants is a key to a successful broadcast.

7

LOOK BEFORE YOU LEAP

Set Your Strategy

SUN TZU

Many people put *The Art of War* by the ancient Chinese general Sun Tzu on the bookshelf in their office. I've seen it in the offices of lawyers, doctors, college presidents, salespeople, even in the lockers of ballplayers. You get a funny feeling when you see it; you go into the office for a meeting, see the big red letters on its spine, and think, wow, this guy is the real article. He must be a true student of strategy!

I once met a client in his office and he had a big leather copy of Machiavelli's *The Prince* sitting prominently on a table. I was a young, impressionable attorney meeting a very wealthy and prominent businessman. I had never read all of *The Prince*, but of course was familiar with its aura. And I thought: wow, this must be a tough customer! A book full of strategies on how to get ahead and stay ahead no matter what. He must be, what's the word, a real Machiavellian strategist!

The *Art of War* and *The Prince* are certainly two credible books on military and political strategy. Superficially, they are about efficiency, ruthlessness, and even deviousness. I learned, however, after my share of strategic mistakes that strategy books—whether classics like these or recent how-to texts—can be misused. They can reinforce the rush to set a strategy rather than formulate one. They can give the impression that you start with strategy rather than build up to one. These books are about what you do when you are faced with a situation rather than how you prepare for what you do. I am not trying to split hairs here. Often you develop a vague objective and then rush to strategy. There are critical steps in between.

All the information you gather via the preparation checklist—your clear objectives, precedents in similar situations, definition of the interests of the other side, forecast outcomes—cohere into a strategy. Strategy is simply the steps you take—one, two, three, four—to achieve your objectives. The word *strategy* has grown too complicated. It has too much of an aura. It has strayed into the realm of expertise and PhDs. Keep it simple: strategy is a set of steps. In fact, even the *Art of War* and *The Prince* can provide precedents and suggest alternatives. The preparation you do dictates the strategy as much as the situation you face. When it comes to preparation and strategy, your focus is on establishing or setting the strategic plan rather than its implementation. Strategic steps are the means to an end. How you prepare or develop those steps will go a long way in determining the level of your success.

SCOWCROFT

In keeping with Sun Tzu's theme, take a look at a quote prior to the second Iraq war from former national security adviser to the first President Bush, Brent Scowcroft. Scowcroft wrote in the *Wall Street Journal* on August 15, 2002:

> Our nation is presently engaged in a debate about whether to launch a war against Iraq. Leaks of various strategies for an attack on Iraq appear with regularity. The Bush administration vows regime change, but states that no decision has been made whether, much less when, to launch an invasion.
>
> It is beyond dispute that Saddam Hussein is a menace. He terrorizes and brutalizes his own people. He has launched war on two of his neighbors. He devotes enormous effort to rebuilding his military forces and equipping them with weapons of mass destruction. We will all be better off when he is gone.
>
> That said, we need to think through this issue very carefully. We need to analyze the relationship between Iraq and our other pressing priorities—notably the war on terrorism—as well as the best strategy and tactics available were we to move to change the regime in Baghdad.

That key last paragraph has stuck with me since I read it. I do not know what went wrong and who did what in the months leading up to the war. You now know far too well, too, who was fired, who was jailed, and who voted for or against the war in Congress, who is pointing fingers at whom. I tried to be a good citizen and understand the whole issue by reading the papers daily, but, frankly, I'm still baffled by how it all happened.

But I am relatively certain about one thing: the post-invasion strategy seems to have been poorly prepared. At least there is consensus on that in both political parties and from most pundits across the political spectrum.

Scowcroft's editorial was significant in part because he had been so loyal to the Bush family for so many years. But his third paragraph here seems written out of concern more than criticism. He is urging the proper formulation of a strategy; he is encouraging the powers that be to slow down and analyze precedents, interests, and alternative outcomes; he agrees with the basic objectives, but stresses that there are steps between the development of objectives and the setting of a strategy. He is saying, in a way, put down Sun Tzu for a while and formulate first. Sun Tzu can come in handy later once a proper strategy is formulated. But keep him on the shelf until you proceed through the steps that will shape a fully informed strategy.

PIZZA BOXES

On a smaller scale, how often have you hung up from a conference call and sat with your team members around the table trying to immediately devise a strategy to confront a new problem? There is a prolonged and increasingly uncomfortable silence until someone says: okay, what's our strategy here?

When we were eager to get new business in the early days of the Shapiro Negotiations Institute, Mark and I did more or less just that. We were looking for distribution channels for our seminars and keynotes, so we quickly targeted speakers' bureaus. We had been told that our presentations were great, so we figured that we could find platforms for them by using speakers' bureaus to pitch us to the corporate world.

To market to the bureaus, our strategy was to send a home-plate-shaped pizza box, stamped with the "Hit a Home Run with Us" theme, to several dozen speakers' bureaus. The boxes contained, in addition to literature on the Institute, baseball trinkets and an autographed ball and minibat. In our minds we were sure that the bureaus would come calling.

Our research on the bureaus had been very limited and we didn't know that the main attractions for them were celebrities and the latest flavor-of-the-day personality—a good approach for them if they were to build their commissions. In short, we didn't study precedents or define the interests of the bureaus. We rushed to set a pizza-box-based strategy.

Not until later did we learn that there were alternatives for distribution that might be more effective for us. So our speakers' bureau campaign ended with few callbacks from the bureaus and some empty pizza boxes left on our shelves.

Our speakers' bureau experience forced us to formulate our strategic plan for distribution more thoroughly. We contacted a corporate training expert who disabused us of our fixation with the bureaus. She suggested selling our services directly to corporate sales and training departments. She also referred us to a "list broker" who provided us with lists of contacts including corporate sales managers and training directors. In short, we developed our own in-house distribution capability. Developing this distribution strategy took time and some methodical planning, but it certainly had its impact: 100 percent growth year after year for the first five years and significant growth since then. In the end, we had executed both strategies successfully, but the real difference maker was the research that went into the creation of the direct distribution strategy. We learned the hard way not to rush to set strategy, but to develop it with prior preparation.

Now whenever someone in my office or even in a seminar asks, "What's our strategy here?," I say we don't have one. The person looks shocked at first, but after a chat soon realizes that you don't start with strategy; you build up to it. Whether you have thirty seconds or three days, you try proceeding through steps that make you an informed strategist. You clarify your objectives; you analyze precedents; you assess the interests of the client or counterpart; you analyze alternative approaches and outcomes; you methodically determine a strategic approach. Our society is so results-oriented that many people just jump to the implementation steps—the strategy—before they take the time to prepare. They forget that gaining an objective or meeting a challenge effectively is a process and not an event.

SLOWING DOWN A GENTLE GIANT

Joe Ehrmann

Joe Ehrmann was a captain of the Baltimore Colts, a stand-out defensive lineman, a mountain of a man. He also grew up tough. His father was physically and mentally abusive. His beloved brother died tragically. His life had a bunch of pain, and he wanted to take its lessons to teach others. So after football, he became a minister, a high school football coach, and a teacher. *Parade Magazine* in a cover story even called him "The Most Important Coach in America."

Joe formed a new entity, Building Men for Others, and went anywhere anytime to deliver his message of empathy, service, and love. He set out to reform the notion of masculinity by emphasizing the importance of relationships and caring communication.

When people would ask him what he charged, Joe would say, "What can you afford?" When he did quote fees, he gave the same answer to the corporate world as to the needier nonprofit world. This might strike you as naïve, but if you knew Joe at the time, you would realize it was simply pure. Joe was so consumed with his need to help others and continue to help himself that he forgot about core financial strategies.

So Joe was out there across the country giving speeches and seminars—for huge discounts compared to what the market would pay. The result was that he might not only have been the best coach in America, but also the lowest-paid and hardest-working speaker in America. Everyone was tapping into his compassionate vein; Joe has such boundless compassion that he even disregarded his own livelihood.

Then the book *Season of Life* came along and Joe became the subject of a bestseller. While Joe helped promote the book by speaking around the country, he wasn't participating in royalties from increased sales of the books. He even promoted the book by signing thousands of copies although he was receiving zero royalties.

One day his wife, Paula, grew so concerned about the toll all his travel and teaching was taking on his health that she intervened. She called me and asked for a sit-down. I had been Joe's agent during his playing days, but we had largely lost contact except for seeing each other at community events and literally passing each other in airports. So we got together and developed a new strategy to help him take into account his financial needs and his family.

"I didn't even think about strategy," Joe said. "I just thought about delivery. So I had to look at the things that prevented me from being strategic—my own pathologies and unresolved issues. The idea of success, of making money, of having an audience kind of overwhelmed me so I postponed all the strategy stuff and just tried to deliver."

Paula and Joe could have rushed into it: corporate advisers were courting Joe with ideas to "commoditize" his image and message. They were really using words like that. They wanted him to structure a business that would build a fortune around his newfound success. But Paula and Joe had learned from their mistakes; they didn't rush into the strategy this time. They looked at Joe's objectives, found precedents for such wholesale marketing that they didn't like, and looked at the interests and needs of his core audience.

We developed a price list tailored to the type of entity—profit or nonprofit—that Joe would work with. We trained a business manager to handle financial discussions so Joe could stay focused on his mission and not have to deal with quoting fees. Subsequently, Joe began to work with Paula and my partner Mark to develop a long-term operational strategy for the business.

"A funny thing happened once I finally set a proper strategy," Joe said. "Not only did I improve my life and focus, but the seminars became more valuable for my audiences. Because I got commitments from ones that could afford them, it was more meaningful and more inclusive. Community groups were forced to partner with each other and not be exclusive. They had to bring in people with money and influence to participate."

Like the newfound strategist Joe Ehrmann, the preparers profiled next in this chapter offer examples of how to formulate and implement strategies and how to adjust them as the circumstances demand. National Public Radio's Liane Hansen gets to the heart of the matter by applying a consistent strategy for interviews. Tom Giannopoulos used a gutsy strategy to grow a small company and deftly adjusted that strategy in the face of unsettling challenges. Lisa Fontenelli of Goldman Sachs uses a consistent strategy for making sense of highly complicated businesses that her research teams cover.

GET TO THE HEART OF THE MATTER

Liane Hansen

Liane Hansen hosts *Weekend Edition Sunday* on National Public Radio. As a listener, you may feel that the questions are just rolling off her tongue, but they really are part of a well-prepared strategy for getting the guest to open up and say something new and insightful. The way she prepares her strategy of probing for information from guests is a clear example of how to get to the heart of the matter whether the situation is an interview, sales call, presentation, or simply dealing with colleagues and bosses at work.

A brush with tragedy helped Liane understand how some journalists can inadequately prepare for interviews and reporting a story. Liane's husband, Neal, was taken hostage in Iraq in 1991 and held for five days. Because of those five awful days of absence in 1991, she is clearer than ever on the proper strategy for probing for the truth beneath the surface of a person or a story.

"I learned firsthand how important it is to remember that you are talking to a person when you are doing an interview," Liane said. "There is so much airtime to fill and so much speculation. The coverage of my husband's situation taught me how imprecise coverage is. Some reports said a journalist—meaning him—had been killed in Basra in a firefight. There was such rampant and unfounded speculation that it was Neal. So I went into reporter mode and came away knowing Neal wasn't dead. But I learned what it was like to be on the receiving end of poor reporting."

As much as the importance of accuracy, those five days in

1991 reinforced that a proper strategy entails grasping for and attempting to convey the full complexity of a person and an issue. Liane's strategy for preparing for an interview is a lesson for anyone trying to get to the bottom of something. She starts with the old list: who, what, when, where, why, and how. She determines the "who, what, when, and where" as any good reporter should, and then digs into the "why" and "how" of the person she is interviewing or the story she is covering. She holds the subject up to the light, gets past the surface, and tries to uncover the how and why of their story.

"My strategy is simply to start with the follow-up question," Liane said. "It is always a better question than the initial question anyway. I like to go for 'how' and 'why' as opposed to rehashing the 'who, what, where, and when.' Those are facts, and they are either obvious or, as I learned with my husband, hard to pin down. The 'how' and 'why' are the way to get people to talk to me as a three-dimensional person."

And so whether she is preparing her strategy to interview the Beatles' producer Sir George Martin or someone who lost a loved one in the crash of Egypt Air 990 in 1999, Liane offers someone in any career an example of formulating the best strategy for getting to the heart of the matter.

Liane uses an anecdote from her interview with the actor Tim Curry on the Sunday morning show to demonstrate getting to "why." She researched several interviews with him in which she noticed his frustration with being asked about starring in *The Rocky Horror Picture Show*. She set her strategy based on her observations.

"I asked him why he doesn't like to talk about it instead of asking him directly about the movie," Liane said. "And we got a great story—the story of his annoyance at being asked by airheads at every little television station around the country about *Rocky Horror*. Asking him why he was bothered led to a whole new story."

To illustrate the effectiveness of focusing on the how, Liane uses the story of preparing to interview a relative of a person who died in the Egypt Air crash. Liane focused on her own precedent—the misinformation in the case of her missing husband—to develop more respectful and provocative questions for family members.

"For news interviews involving people's families, you especially have to get away from speculation," Liane explained. "This applies to war hostages or airplane crashes. It also is unfair to call a family member and ask 'how do you feel?'" It also leads to a poor answer that is roughly the same over and over. You can't sufficiently answer that question. So instead I ask 'how are you coping?' I asked that during Egypt Air and got this incredibly human story about neighbors constantly coming over to give their support. It ended up giving more insight into the tragedy than any other question."

Preparation by means of the how and why can indeed lead to moments of insight and poignancy that one might never have expected. Liane was once one of many reporters interviewing Sir George Martin, the legendary producer for the Beatles. He was getting the questions that most reporters assumed the audience wanted to hear—about working with the Beatles, best songs, what could have been if they had stayed together. But Liane prepared by listening to hours of recording and reading stories from decades ago.

And she was struck by a new way to probe for the core of the story. She knew that Sir George was losing his hearing. And she knew that, from his perspective, this impairment would change his story of the Beatles forever.

"Here is a guy who has made his living listening, using his ears," Liane said. "You can't ask 'how does it feel to lose your hearing?' But, as with the airline families, you can ask 'how do you cope with the fact that you made your living listening and now that is more difficult?' And he let down all his guards and talked about how he had always seen music in colors and even saw Paul blue, John red, and so on. The interview became about how he sees music."

Liane's devotion to probing also can lead her to utilize the oldest and simplest technique in the book: silence. As a student of her art, Liane has noticed that preparing to interject silence or pauses at timely moments in an interview can lead to great revelations.

"There is a real tendency in media for it to all be about the person doing the asking," Liane noted. "You can see when hosts love it when guests say 'Oh, that's a good question.' But I think the less said by me, the better. The guest is there to talk. The best question is sometimes silence. Nature abhors a vacuum, so most people will leap in to fill it."

Silence as the most penetrating question; that is certainly a minimalist technique. But Liane demonstrates that strategy is a subtle thing. She returns to the basics of probing—the how and the why. She minimizes herself. Her strategy usually leads to new insight.

Her preparation—searching for the most current and basic story in Sir George Martin's life or using her own experience as she searched for hope while her husband was missing—shows the strategic artistry involved in getting to the heart of the matter. She looks before she leaps into an interview.

THE TECHNOLOGY STRATEGIST

Tom Giannopoulos

Tom Giannopoulos, CEO of Micros Systems since 1993, has transformed the company into a leading information technology supplier for the hospitality and retail industries. He has made key acquisitions, surrounded himself with savvy management, and used spartan determination as part of his strategy for growth. Tom offers an example of how to prepare a strategy when unforeseen events thwart the best-laid plans.

Tom dreamed of becoming an engineer when he was in high school. But Greece had a struggling economy in the post–World War II doldrums. There was one university, and fifteen out of three thousand applicants to the engineering program were accepted each year.

So Tom decided to cross the seas to find the education that he wanted at Lamar University in Texas. He landed a job at the then mighty Westinghouse. Tom thrived there until the late 1980s when Westinghouse's revenue began to decline as the cold war thawed and defense budgets were reduced. Westinghouse determined that it had to move into segments of the technology industry beyond defense. As part of its strategy, Westinghouse purchased Micros, then a small company focused on providing technology to restaurants, and made Tom the point person for meshing the two entities.

Tom went from jointly working for the two companies to taking Micros public as CEO in 1996 when Westinghouse sold its controlling interest.

Micros's ascent in its industry and its popularity in the capital markets can be explained by Tom's diversifying Micros's client base. Micros started selling the same technology platform to casinos, hotels, and clothing stores as well as acquiring companies focused on those fields.

"We knew early on that it was critical for us to expand our software and services into hotel and into retail," Tom said. "If you are going to be a player in an industry, you have to be a player in all segments with products that are basically complementary across subindustries. We immediately started to look for a company in the hotel segment with products that were complementary in addressing hotel reservations software, rates, availability, inventory across all hotels in the chain, guest profiles, and the like. Our strategy was to refine and improve our restaurant software and look for companies in related service fields that we understood because of our expertise."

But Micros's first big acquisition in the hospitality field, a German hotel software company, Fidelio, did not go according to plan. Fidelio helped Micros fulfill Tom's vision for rapid growth, and the company's leadership was well respected and very connected throughout Europe. When they departed soon after the purchase, Tom was left with a hollowed-out brand. The Fidelio product was still superior, but he had lost its founding symbols and risked losing the customer relationships that Fidelio took with it. Investors were urging him to shed the acquisition.

So Tom began to prepare a strategy to meet the sudden challenge.

"I went to Munich for six weeks and interviewed all the employees of the company," Tom said. "I spent a lot of the time visiting all their customers all over Europe to determine what they were and weren't happy with. We had many meetings with the remaining Fidelio management team to assess product development and customer service issues."

Tom spent the time required to understand his market's interests. He left Europe with the information essential to prepare a new strategy for Fidelio. He met with his key management team in the United States and determined that a trilingual, experienced manager they had identified in Europe could take Fidelio to a new level. Based on what Tom had learned from his research, Micros also moved Fidelio's headquarters to a cheaper location in Germany. Micros used the savings and its new self-awareness to increase staffing and improve customer service. Thus, Tom turned a disruption to his growth strategy into the opportunity to prepare a new and even better strategy for what they now called Micros Fidelio.

Having recovered from the Fidelio fiasco, Micros's growth started to skyrocket. Then the terrorist attacks of September 11, 2001, devastated the hospitality and leisure industries. Micros felt the brunt of the economic fallout because its clients—hotels, restaurants, and other leisure destinations—suffered along with airline companies. The very field Tom was diversifying into was buckling. Some rivals among the technology companies that serviced these industries sold off assets, cut budgets for software research and development, and significantly reduced payroll. Some went bankrupt.

The whole mess occurred as Micros's product cycle was winding down. It was preparing to replace the existing systems it provided to companies with a new system—something that happens every seven to ten years as software gets developed and improved. To prepare his company to deal with the crisis, Tom and his team asked themselves fundamental questions.

Tom said, "2003 would have been the year when updates would occur. In 2001, we had development engineers who were a year from concluding and testing the new products. So do we slow down the development or continue with the developers in place and on the same schedule regardless of the slowdown? We analyzed the industry and the overall economy; we looked at our hotel customers and large food venues and determined with them that business funding would return faster than from a normal economic slowdown. At Micros we needed to have product ready a year later to maintain our revenue growth. We convinced our customers the best thing was for them to stay committed to the new product to increase revenue stream as well."

Tom's approach—honing his strategy but maintaining its overall thrust—contradicted the majority of companies in his industry. Like Bill Miller of Legg Mason on the investment side, Tom prepared by analyzing precedents in the business and determined that the industries tended to overcome singular shocks better than economic-based slowdowns. He more clearly defined the interests of his clients and educated them about alternative outcomes to the situation they were facing.

Micros had to make cuts, but Tom did it in a way that allowed for Micros to pursue his refined strategy for expanding market share once the industries recovered. He trimmed marketing and other overhead costs, but dedicated a greater proportion of revenue to research and development.

"We made a strategic decision to reduce head count in all areas except product development," Tom said. "We determined that this slowdown offered an opportunity to create new products and refine preexisting ones. We kept full funding for our research and development for hotels and restaurants and captured more market share because of it. It was a strategic decision that paid off."

Tom's inclination to adjust strategy rather than abandon it is likely related to an old-fashioned Greek steadfastness in his blood. Tom's experience at Micros demonstrates that taking the time to adjust a strategy in the face of challenging events is done best if it is done as methodically as the initial setting of that strategy.

THE PARTS OF THE WHOLE

Lisa Fontenelli

Lisa Fontenelli is a partner at Goldman Sachs and the chief operating officer of the Global Investment Research division.

As a former analyst, Lisa's success on Wall Street is based on preparing a strategy for understanding and monitoring the innumerable moving parts in a company's business model. The steps she takes to assemble her research and form an opinion on the value of a company demand a level of accuracy that comes from her strategy of breaking complex challenges into smaller parts.

I am going to focus more on Lisa's work as a securities analyst than on her current role at Goldman Sachs. Lisa says she always thought the position should be called "insecurities analyst." That is, she realized that you have to be just insecure enough to always worry about what you might be missing. An equity security's market value is constantly affected by changes in each link of the company's value chain as well as changes in economic and market forces. Lisa and her team tracked numerous moving pieces that comprise the fundamentals of a company, its competitors, its suppliers, and its customers. Lisa primarily covered U.S.-based manufacturers, and she researched and tracked every part of the value chain—material parts, labor, manufacturing, production lines, transport, marketing—that led to the sale of the final product.

Preparation is indeed partially driven by insecurity, at least in my experience. The insecurities can be personal or professional, but they usually result in the pursuit of a perfectionism that drives preparation. Great preparers anticipate what can go wrong and do as much as they can to prevent it. The stakes are high on Wall Street, and poor research can be costly to a company or a career. As Lisa noted, it is not possible to be right 100 percent of the time; failure or error is always right around the corner. Lisa openly acknowledges her fair share of "getting it wrong," but she believes that learning from your mistakes is part of a continuous improvement process.

"I realized early on that there is really no moment in this

business when things settle," Lisa said. "Macro- and micro-economic factors, productivity improvements in the manu-facturing process, timing contingencies all create flux. A strategy for research that aims to identify opportunities for the creation or destruction of value has to be built on that recognition."

Lisa's office is high up in a building at the tip of Manhat-tan. From one window you see the convergence of the East River and New York Harbor. From the other you see Ellis Island. Big cargo ships are lined up to deliver their goods to one of the biggest ports in the world. Lisa and her team probably researched some of the companies whose prod-ucts or parts fill those ships. Even the fickleness of the sea or paperwork at the port can undermine the supply chain.

To channel the insecurity inherent in her work, Lisa pre-pares a very clear strategy for how to approach, perform, and continuously update her research. That preparation en-tails focusing on the parts more than the whole. That is, she and her team diligently track each piece of the value chain before implementing an investment strategy that addresses the effect on a company's bottom line.

"My strategy has always been to understand the value chain," Lisa said. "In the value chain of a consumer products company, new product generation is paramount, so learning the R&D process is the first step. Then understanding the method and cost from procurement of raw materials to the manufacturing process, efficiency of equipment, and need to make capital investment; you ask where and how they ware-house and what are their logistics for transport and delivery. You also have to recognize that for consumer products companies, often "customer" and "consumer" are two different concepts. You have to know how they are merchandizing to retail stores and how the stores are advertising to the consumers who buy from the stores. To close the loop, you have to monitor sales by product line, which is the measure of consumer behavior that feeds back into R&D. Only then can you make forecasts for earnings and cash flow, which can then be discounted back to determine whether a security is over- or undervalued."

Okay. Got that? The only way that a human being could ever keep track of all that is by staying devoted to constant preparation. Lisa is a master at simplifying. She shapes her strategy of breaking a whole into its parts, and then lets that strategy carry her through the process that leads to an informed investment decision.

KEY POINTS

STRATEGY

- Strategy—setting the steps you will take—is too often the first step in people's preparation. The rush to set strategy often leads to a hollow or misguided plan.

- Strategy should be the result of methodical preparation, not the starting point. The process of the preparation principles leads to the formulation of an informed strategy.

- After you set your strategy, then your team, timeline, and script (the final three principles) help you hone it and set the stage for its execution.

- A skillful interviewer, Liane Hansen researches the "who, what, when, and where" of a story and then deftly but relentlessly sets a strategy for finding the "why and how" from her guests. The result is a more informative and interesting encounter.

- Unexpected events often force you to adjust your strategy. Be it the departure of a key leadership team or 9/11's jolt to his industry, Tom Giannopoulos prepares to adjust his strategy as methodically as he prepared to set it in the first place.

- To give an accurate evaluation of a manufacturing company, Lisa Fontenelli has to constantly monitor the numerous moving parts of its production process. Her strategy for simplifying complexity applies to any project with multiple and changing components.

8

WHEN THE RUBBER MEETS THE ROAD

Do a Timeline

Imagine the Battle of Normandy if the strategy of the invasion were not governed by a timeline. Although temperamental weather affected how that timeline unfolded, the coordination of the Allied forces and their numerous challenges demanded a careful mapping out of the steps of the invasion and when they would occur.

While few of us face the magnitude of the challenge of a military invasion, most of the challenges we face can be met with the same effectiveness as Normandy if we take the time to develop a timeline—a simple graph, list, or chart with projected dates or time frames lined up alongside key steps or milestones.

I developed a sense of the importance of a timeline in my days as a securities/corporate lawyer. Whether I was working on a public offering of stock or a merger, the filing and other regulatory deadlines forced us to prepare a list of assignments and deadlines or completion dates to ensure the transaction's success.

The lawyers, accountants, company officials, printers, and legal assistants would all collaborate and coordinate their roles in the transaction so the deals would get done on time. A common timeline that we distributed and updated guided us through the maze of all the arduous paperwork and required submissions.

If you are not a securities lawyer or a general coordinating an invasion, you may hesitate to undertake a timeline because it is not traditionally done in your business or for the challenge you face. You may just say you don't have time for writing timelines—you can imagine the steps in your head.

Or you may even dread that timelines will be used against you. A timeline invites scrutiny that is often far too facile. For example, I have a friend who is a project manager for a real estate development company. Part of the company's routine is for him to meet his boss once a week to give a project update. The subject of each meeting is the budget and timeline. Because the boss is not engaged on a day-to-day basis with the obstacles that affect timelines, he does not understand why there may be delays. Indeed, a running joke among project managers at the company is the reaction of the boss to delays. The project managers do their time-lines halfheartedly because of the feeling that it will be held against them.

But take a moment to consider four reasons why time-lines, when properly treated, are an invaluable step in tying up your project preparation.

First, the mere exercise of writing a timeline instills a sense of trajectory into your work. Momentum is as critical in business as in sports, and as you complete each mile-stone you develop the psychological benefit of momentum like a tennis player winning successive games or sets.

Second, the timeline becomes a good source for collabo-ration. It instills a sense of teamwork into an undertaking. The deadline becomes the opponent, or the time to beat, or the scoreboard, and you can use it in a way that builds a sense of challenge and teamwork. Milestones motivate.

Third, on the most practical level, we all know that projects can take on a life of their own unless you control the time factor. Without a timeline, you may find yourself unable to move the project along to meet real or conceptual deadlines. A timeline is a vital step as you prepare to control the course of a project and not let it control you. Without one you may even end up going on beyond a logical or appropriate stopping point and thereby consume time that might have better been used on other challenges.

And fourth, a timeline may be a good vehicle for fleshing out how to accomplish tasks. The act of writing a timeline encourages you to brainstorm the steps required to suc-ceed. By laying out your milestones in a row, you can shake out new steps, envision contingencies, or even develop new strategies that you otherwise might not have considered. And, despite a timeline's great value, it's the preparation principle that often takes the least amount of time.

Think about a Springsteen concert and the E Street Band's confidence. I bet that the set list and even each foray into the crowd are prepared down to the minute. The result is a seamless and usually peerless rock show. View your timeline as your set list. Your performance will be more confident and clear.

A common criticism of timelines is that they inevitably go off track. Certainly the weather and the difficulty of assembling landing craft delayed the planned D-day invasion from May to June 6. And I've had a securities offering or two in which market conditions forced us to revamp the schedule. Over the course of my career, I reckon that a minority of my tasks stay true to their timeline. Some tasks beat their projected milestones and time frame; most take detours that erode early timeline projections. Some resistance to doing timelines arises because of this inevitable slippage. But look at it another way: make examples of timeline slippage a precedent item whenever you proceed through the preparation checklist to prepare for a task. Also, there is nothing wrong with variations or time-outs. It is important to not look at deviations from timelines as flaws or failures.

Timelines are not measurements of success and failure; they are mere road maps and organizing tools. So if you are proceeding step-by-step on your timeline in a more or less timely fashion, you are succeeding. The structure, collaboration, and motivation that timelines can generate should be the point, not a lockstep fixation with their predictive accuracy.

. . .

Next in this chapter, you'll read about how Wendy Webster of Wegmans gets a business and its team up and running by guiding the process with a timeline. Television executive Arnie Kleiner used a timeline to transform the technological infrastructure of his station without disrupting operations. Political consultant and campaign manager Larry Gibson used timelines to coordinate the complex international components of a history-making election. All three show how timelines can help teams cohere. But I think, more important, all three show that timelines do not have to be drudgery; in each case they are exhilarating parts of preparation.

OPENING ON TIME

Wendy Webster

If you have ever walked into a spacious and elegant supermarket like Wegmans on its first day of operation, you feel the excitement of a premiere. Getting a Wegmans store opened on time requires devotion to a demanding timeline of tasks that also provides its own kind of rush to the Wegmans team. Wendy Webster, a manager for Wegmans, shows how preparing with a timeline can help get a business up and running despite the daunting demands of numerous moving parts. The night before game day, Wendy Webster visualizes the grand opening: people rush into a store the size of four football fields, her team is masterfully answering questions about rare cheeses and organic meats, and local politicians and food banks are marveling at the result of their collaboration with the new Wegmans super-store.

The morning arrives and Wendy feels the adrenaline in her blood. The crowd is massing at the doors; Wendy does one last walk-through; she holds a brief meeting with her department managers; she fills her cup with coffee for the third time and checks her watch; she gives the sign to open the doors to a new Wegmans and trusts that two years of preparation will yield the results that she visualized the night before.

A Wegmans opening matches any big opening night in terms of fan appreciation. Communities treat the store like royalty as it arrives. But the preparation requires a level of methodical preparation years in advance that reminds me of Eric Mangini laying out every day of his coaching staff's calendar even in the off-season.

"We are not in the grocery business but in the people business," Wendy said. "I played a lot of sports growing up and the preparation of a team is what this is all about. And you need a good timeline that coordinates hundreds of moving parts to do that."

Indeed, as one of Wegmans's key store openers, Wendy manages two timelines that have to intersect as opening day approaches. First, she is building and training her team, negotiating with local entities, and managing public relations on one timeline. And on the other, she is constantly interacting with the Wegmans construction manager to track progress and make sure that the two timelines dovetail prior to opening.

Based on her experience opening four Wegmans, Wendy developed a manual that covers every topic and contingency imaginable, and she constantly updates each timeline and reviews them weekly with her key team members. On a wall in her office she has names of job candidates that she updates much like the general manager of an NFL team preparing for the annual draft of college players.

As she sits in the café overlooking the entire store in Hunt Valley, Maryland, Wendy watches the teeming shoppers push their carts through the layout of fresh fruits and vegetables from around the world. The floor is bustling; the variety and color and scents of the products seems to lift people out of themselves.

"They are an old-fashioned tool, but timelines work," Wendy said. "The preparation that goes into an opening is so vast that you have to do it in a coordinated way. The manual really guides you through the milestones on the timeline, and we have a great team to provide support in all areas."

In terms of her construction timeline, Wendy and Wegmans leadership first must identify the location of a suitable construction office near the site. Wendy likes to have it within view of the site so that there is a visual reference when the team timeline meetings occur.

The construction piece is managed directly by Wegmans's own construction manager. He prepares for contingencies such as roofing supplies not arriving on time because of bad weather; the health inspector demanding to reinspect a water line; the fire marshal seeing the back door propped open one day on a surprise visit. The construction manager and Wendy work so closely that each knows the other's business as well as most project managers in either trade. And they get backup from a coordinator at the Wegmans headquarters in upstate New York who constantly assesses the joint timelines.

"The staffing and stocking of the store occurs side by side with construction, so I attend all those meetings from day one," Wendy said.

Since construction usually takes twenty-four months, Wendy begins her store timeline by setting up local infrastructure. The first step is establishing a hiring office near the construction site so job candidates and the Wegmans team can see the store taking shape. Wendy and her staff also set up training rooms for customer service, safety, and computer training. She identifies and begins coordination with the local food banks to supply them with excess product. She develops alliances with local workforce initiatives and nonprofits. And she negotiates with local officials on issues like the provision of public transportation for her new team and for customers alike.

"There are different challenges whenever we go into a new state," Wendy said. "We have to build that into our timeline so we familiarize ourselves early on in the preparation process. For example, laws for our type of business are done county by county in Maryland but in Virginia they are statewide. So here in Maryland I had to figure out the network and the laws up front."

With eighteen months to go, Wendy starts to build her version of a pro football draft board. She literally fills a wall with cards that track candidates, interview results, offers, and acceptances for every position in every department in the store.

"My wall is really a big part of my timeline," Wendy said. "It is the first thing I review each day. I set a goal every week

WENDY WEBSTER'S WEGMANS TIMELINE

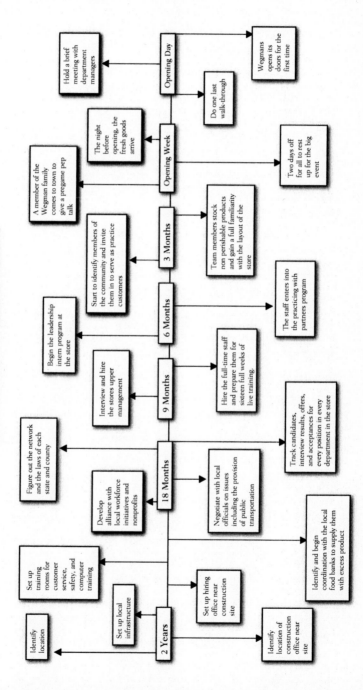

Opening Day
- Hold a brief meeting with department managers
- Do one last walk-through
- Wegmans opens its doors for the first time

Opening Week
- The night before opening, the fresh goods arrive
- A member of the Wegman family comes to town to give a pregame pep talk
- Two days off for all to rest up for the big event

3 Months
- Team members stock non perishable products and gain a full familiarity with the layout of the store
- Start to identify members of the community and invite them in to serve as practice customers

6 Months
- Begin the leadership intern program at the store
- The staff enters into the practicing with partners program

9 Months
- Interview and hire the stores upper management
- Hire the full-time staff and prepare them for sixteen full weeks of live training.

18 Months
- Figure out the network and the laws of each state and county
- Develop alliance with local workforce initiatives and nonprofits
- Negotiate with local officials on issues including the provision of public transportation
- Track candidates, interview results, offers, and acceptances for every position in every department in the store

2 Years
- Identify location
- Set up training rooms for customer service, safety, and computer training
- Set up local infrastructure
- Set up hiring office near construction site
- Identify location of construction office near site
- Identify and begin coordination with the local food banks to supply them with excess product

for my hires. When you know you have found a good person, you hire them even if it means carrying them for a year. I build my training budget to allow for this."

With nine months to go, Wendy has interviewed and hired the store's entire upper management.

With six months to go, she has hired the entire full-time staff and is preparing them for sixteen full weeks of live training. Some of that will occur at the training center for the new site, and some will be done at Wegmans stores around the country.

Wendy also begins the leadership intern program at the store. She starts to get a sense of which new staff members show the qualities that will make them a good team leader for, say, fruits and vegetables or dairy. These team leaders start to become trainers as much as trainees at this point: Wendy encourages them to participate in the actual training of the team even before they have completed their own training.

At this juncture, the entire staff also enters into the so-called practicing with partners program. Wendy and headquarters collaborate to assign each trainee to practice with an existing Wegmans employee at stores around the country.

"It is very important that they train at an existing store," Wendy said. "We try to let them pick the store, put them in hotels, and really integrate them into a functioning operation and into the customer experience. Some travel for six to nine months."

With two weeks to go, the practicing with partners program adds a new, and even more important partner, selected community members. Three months before the opening Wendy and her staff had identified these individuals and invited them to serve as practice customers. They now come onboard with two weeks remaining. That way, her staff completes its training on its home turf instead of in far-flung stores across the country.

Finally, with three days to go, members of the Wegman family come to town to give a pregame pep talk. In the weeks leading up to this, team members have stocked non-perishable products and they have gained a full familiarity with the layout of the store. The night before opening, the fresh goods arrive.

"This is a private company, still a family company in many ways," Wendy said. "We instill that message throughout the timeline, but like to end the timeline with a direct communication. I was privileged to see Mr. Wegman do one of his final programs before he died. That really motivates the team."

The final step in her timeline is rest before the storm. Wendy gives everyone the final two days off to rest up for the big event.

By sticking true to this preparation method and timeline, Wendy wins the game. But opening day is only the first day of an endless season, and many of the same timeline techniques still serve the store well now that it is up and running.

"Wegmans is a preparation culture," Wendy said about a company that is regularly voted by employees as among the best employers in America. "I was a huge preparer all my life, but here they give you a stronger background and methodology. The whole structure that guides the opening of a store is founded on thorough preparation and that I think carries over into operations."

Proof of the carryover might be the booming business

that almost all Wegmans stores continue to do after the initial community excitement about an opening. Adherence to a well-prepared timeline is a critical part of each Wegmans store's foundation.

TIMELINES ON TELEVISION

Arnie Kleiner

Preparing with a timeline can be the fine line between keeping a business operating without disruption and losing the public's confidence altogether, as the story of Arnie Kleiner and ABC-7 in Los Angeles makes clear.

Arnie, the head of ABC-7, does not sleep much. He usually wakes up on the hour, looks at his alarm clock—his nocturnal timeline—and reviews his critical tasks timeline in his head for the next day. Then his thoughts turn to the timeline of critical projects for the station, including the relocation of their studios or the conversion of their technology to high-definition format. Arnie lives and breathes timelines more than anyone I know.

Arnie's business has undergone incredible technological change in the past decade. At sixty-four, Arnie could use his age as an excuse to let others deal with this challenge. But he leads one of the most technologically advanced and largest local television stations in the United States for two reasons: he knows how to manage people, and he knows how to make people and projects cohere around a timeline.

"It's really that old trick about hiring people you know can do the job and then letting them do it," Arnie says. "The only thing I throw in is that they know that when they tell me they will have a job done on a certain date, I want it on that date and I want to see the steps laid out along a timeline to get us there. You have to think about the nature of our business—it is all about deadlines, starting shows on time, moving to get a story, and delivering it as fast as you can."

Timelines drove two major overhauls at his station. The first was a physical overhaul and relocation of the entire station; the second was the overhaul of the technology and staffing of ABC-7's production room. ABC-7 until 2000 was a scattered hodgepodge of studios and offices. It was an incredibly effective channel serving one of the largest and most diverse audiences in the world, but its physical chaos undermined its production efficiency.

"We were on an old movie lot for fifty years," Arnie said with his hearty laugh regularly interrupting his vivid recollection. "It was an old Hollywood studio lot, and *General Hospital* people and various production services were running all around it alongside us. The station itself was housed in seven different buildings. The newsroom and the studio were two blocks away from headquarters. You had to climb down fire escape steps and sneak up alleyways to arrive to very critical places. And fundamentally it was so hard to know who worked for you. There were fifteen hundred people on the lot. One of the first things I did was put up a picture board near the commissary so we could know our colleagues weren't extras on a soap show."

So Arnie and the station's owner, Disney, began the search for a more appropriate space. The only problem was that everyone realized immediately the devastating complications of relocating a television station. ABC-7 runs forty and a half hours of local news each week: two hours in the early morning, an hour at midday, two and a half hours in the early evening, a half hour at night, and four hours on Sunday morning. That is a lot of footage, a lot of airtime, and a lot of loyal viewers to keep entertained and interested. In his business, given fickle viewer loyalty and critical advertising revenue, Arnie could not afford to lose a minute of airtime, let alone the week or two needed to relocate that would strike any industry outsider as reasonable.

"We realized early that the only way to achieve this was going to be to set very specific timelines for every piece of the puzzle," Arnie said. "I engaged my staff not from the top down but from the bottom up. I told them to tell me what was reasonable for planning, packing, and moving each of their divisions or sections. Then I scrutinized them, not necessarily pushing back but making sure they were realistic. I could tolerate a long process. But I couldn't deal with delays. We had to tie together so many different timelines that one going awry would blow up the whole process."

Take a look at the next page to get a sense of the complexity of the move of ABC-7.

And you thought that planning for the Normandy invasion was complicated. During and soon after the move, ABC-7 also began a complete overhaul of its technology, becoming one of the first high-definition local stations in the country, as well as the largest.

Now, how on earth did so many moving parts cohere on a specific day at a specific place? Arnie loves to talk about how many station employees would come in on their days off just to watch this great choreography take place.

"I had set timeline goals for myself, then went through the

ARNIE KLEINER'S TIMELINE

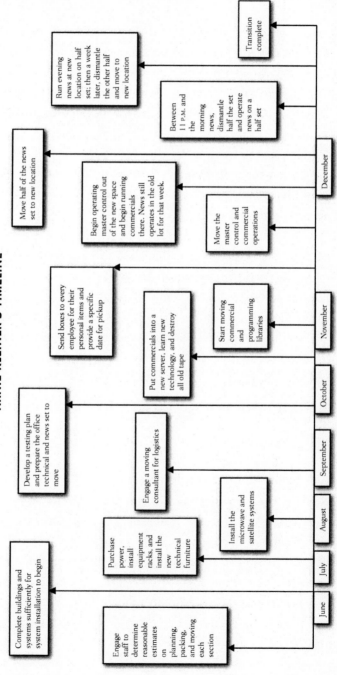

process of asking people to set their own goals," Arnie said. "If I found their answers to be reasonable but not what I wanted, I would still side with them. If I felt they were stringing me along, I would go with my date or time frame. Then I plotted everything together on paper with my top managers. We reviewed the timeline at least twice a week during a special meeting. Of course we made some adjustments, but the overall timeline was met. Otherwise there would have been huge costs—advertising loss, overtime, mover contracts."

So if you are like me and think you could probably never learn from or even have any interest in the relocation of a television studio, I hope you are thinking twice now.

Arnie and ABC-7 provide an example of what preparation with timelines can do for organizations and careers. They may seem arduous and irritating, but in the right hands timelines can become elegant and reassuring.

A TIMELINE FOR SAVING LIBERIA

Larry Gibson

Electing the president of a country is a complicated task. A timeline makes that seemingly impossible job more manageable and in one recent case helped to make history with the election of Ellen Johnson Sirleaf as president of Liberia in 2005. Larry Gibson, a former associate deputy attorney general of the United States and campaign manager for former Baltimore mayor Kurt Schmoke, advised Sirleaf, and she is now the country's greatest hope for not suffering a relapse of its interminable civil war.

The story of her election is in large part the story of a timeline. If you think you have difficulty sticking to a timeline on a project, imagine doing it in Liberia, an impoverished country, obliterated by war, and heedless to time in a hopeless sort of way.

As Ellen Johnson Sirleaf's campaign planner, Larry installed a timeline (see the next page) and consequently helped instill hope that an election could finally change things for the better. He also addressed some old grief: one of Larry's close friends, C. Cecil Dennis, then Liberia's foreign minister, was killed by rebels in a firing squad at the start of the civil war twenty-five years ago.

On his first trip to Liberia after a twenty-seven-year absence, Larry conducted a feasibility assessment for Sirleaf's long-shot campaign. The last words of his written report to Sirleaf were: "Opportunity plus preparation equal success." Larry's timeline guided that preparation.

Larry determined that the best way to perform the first step on his timeline, a feasibility study, was to do it himself. To give a complete opinion, he needed the complete picture firsthand. No hiring Western polling groups, no fancy technology. Just hit the road and see what the people are saying. He traveled through Liberia for two weeks with a driver and a guide. He kept introducing himself to as many people as he could talk to as simply Professor Larry Gibson of the University of Maryland School of Law. He didn't identify himself with the campaign so as not to taint people's attitudes toward his candidate.

Larry found that about 80 percent of his interviewees said that education was the most important qualification for a candidate; 15 percent said the candidate's experience;

LARRY GIBSON'S TIMELINE

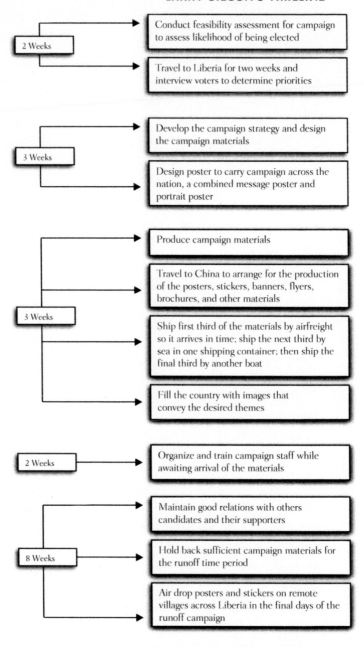

2 Weeks
- Conduct feasibility assessment for campaign to assess likelihood of being elected
- Travel to Liberia for two weeks and interview voters to determine priorities

3 Weeks
- Develop the campaign strategy and design the campaign materials
- Design poster to carry campaign across the nation, a combined message poster and portrait poster

3 Weeks
- Produce campaign materials
- Travel to China to arrange for the production of the posters, stickers, banners, flyers, brochures, and other materials
- Ship first third of the materials by airfreight so it arrives in time; ship the next third by sea in one shipping container; then ship the final third by another boat
- Fill the country with images that convey the desired themes

2 Weeks
- Organize and train campaign staff while awaiting arrival of the materials

8 Weeks
- Maintain good relations with others candidates and their supporters
- Hold back sufficient campaign materials for the runoff time period
- Air drop posters and stickers on remote villages across Liberia in the final days of the runoff campaign

5 percent said platform; and no one said the candidate's party was important. This was a shocking and important discovery at the outset of his timeline. Liberia, Larry realized, was so exhausted by its civil war that party politics, normally a major factor in African elections, no longer mattered. Political parties reminded people of the divisions that the civil war fed upon. He immediately saw strength in Sirleaf's stellar educational credentials, with three degrees from U.S. universities, including Harvard. On the basis of his interviews, he determined that she stood a chance.

One last issue, though, was her gender. The civil war was primarily a male event, and something along the lines of the rebellion of the women in the Greek play *Lysistrata* was taking place in Liberia. Larry found women across the country who said, "Men have failed us and they are too violent." Many women expressed the view that men should step back from the stage since they had been at one another's throats for twenty-five years. He even found that a surprising number of men held the same opinion: "I knew at that moment the bottom-line conclusion of my feasibility study."

The next steps on his timeline were developing the campaign strategy and designing the campaign materials. Larry allowed himself three weeks for this essential work. His designs included the poster which was both a message poster and a portrait poster, that would carry Sirleaf's campaign across the nation.

"I was in Ellen's house one day and saw an old picture in a frame on the floor," Larry said. "We were struggling, about to get off-track on our timeline. We just couldn't come up with the imagery that felt right. Then I saw that photo out of the corner of my eye. Ellen was being let out of jail in 1986 and was defiantly raising her fist in the air. I had Ellen pose for a new photo with her giving the same gesture with hand raised. Then I juxtaposed the young Ellen and the Ellen of today on a single poster." That poster with 1986 and 2005 images of Ellen Johnson Sirleaf became the "message" poster of the campaign.

The next milestone on his timeline, the actual production of the campaign materials, provided the most challenging time frame for Larry, because it required transcontinental coordination.

Larry traveled to China and arranged for the production of the posters, stickers, banners, flyers, and brochures, and other materials. That was the easy part.

"Getting the material back to Liberia was the hard part." Larry said. "We did not have enough time for the first shipment to come by boat. So I staggered it—we sent the first third of the materials by much more expensive airfreight, the next third by sea in one shipping container, then the final third by another boat. If the airfreight portion had been just two days late, we would have missed the critical opening of the campaign period and would never have recovered."

The campaign staff was organized and trained while awaiting arrival of the materials, which came right on schedule. Then, armed with tons of paper and glue, push brooms, tape, staple guns, T-shirts, and banners, the campaign bombarded the country with images of Ellen that conveyed the desired themes.

But Larry had made a critical decision to hold back some of the materials. His feasibility study gave him the confidence to bet that no candidate would get a majority on the first round and that there would be a runoff between the top two vote getters. He urged Sirleaf and her partisans to maintain good relations with other candidates and their supporters. He preached that they be considered "not enemies, but just players on a different team." Losing candidates and their supporters would later be valuable allies in the runoff election. Larry added the runoff time period to his timeline and held back campaign materials for this period at the end of his timeline. Many people in the campaign, eager to win on the first round of voting, questioned the extension of the timeline to include this runoff. But Larry turned out to be right.

The leading candidate in the first round, former European soccer player of the year George Weah, distributed all his materials and spent all of his funds. Larry used his timeline to pace Ellen's campaign efforts and investments to a comfortable win in the runoff election.

In the final days of the runoff campaign, using a technique Larry had witnessed in a 2001 election campaign in Madagascar, the Sirleaf campaign used a rented helicopter to drop thousands of posters and stickers on two hundred remote villages across Liberia.

Ellen Johnson Sirleaf—a younger, defiant version alongside an older, mature one in traditional African dress—was literally "falling from the sky" across Liberia. Even the heavens appeared to be on her side.

Timelines, when used creatively and with nuance, can make for magical moments like this. Larry Gibson, for all his soulfulness and nonchalance, knows that such magic can come from rigid devotion to tracking project milestones. And something so basic as a timeline can help guide the complex process of transforming a country.

KEY POINTS

TIMELINES

- Timelines can be viewed as drudgery. Because of an inadequate understanding of their impact, they are often disregarded as simplistic or, on the other hand, too cumbersome and destined to fail.

- But timelines are really nothing more than an organizational tool and a way to guide and test your vision of a project. You may or may not meet the dates aligned with the milestones on your timeline, but the sheer process is part of preparation. Timelines are not your taskmaster—they're a vehicle to clarify your preparation in general and your strategy in particular.

- The point is that you are thinking through the steps that form the strategy you have set to fulfill your objectives.

- Wendy Webster uses timelines as a tool to organize complicated store openings that would otherwise succumb to chaos without the regular review of milestones by team members.

- Arnie Kleiner uses timelines to help his team collaborate better. He does not view them so much as tools for evaluating performance but as a means for improving collaborative performance.

- Larry Gibson uses timelines to inform and strengthen his strategy. He lays out his strategic steps on a timeline, reviews them with his team, and refines or adjusts his strategy for winning elections accordingly.

9

THE RIGHT PARTS FOR
THE RIGHT PEOPLE

Pick Your Team

Working as a team can be tough to do in many organizations. Personal rivalries, deadlines, too much to do and not enough time to do it—so many factors prevent you from forming relationships with colleagues so you can rely on each other to exchange ideas, critiques, and support.

It does not have to be this way. A quality of top-notch professionals, and especially top preparers, is a willingness to collaborate with talented colleagues. Preparing for success in today's transactional world—be it leading a pharmaceutical company or operating a pharmacy, developing a building or selling a house, legislating change or litigating a case—demands that you prepare by properly allocating responsibilities among your team. Who on your team does what and how do you decide this?

A team helps build your knowledge base, broadens your vision, and provides the essential opportunity to use devil's advocates. A key part of preparation is knowing your different team members' skills and matching those skills to appropriate parts of your game plan.

For example, Jill is especially effective at selling deals when she can build on a relationship that is already established. She is not used for cold call selling because Jack thrives on breaking through to customers with whom there has been no prior contact.

Picking the right team member with whom to develop an idea or a script is also a critical part of preparation. Think of how rock bands fly in top-notch producers to take their records to a new level. Think about how certain top authors insist on working with particular editors. Your devil's advocates can take your preparation to another level. Preparation partners bring a new perspective to the process that the preparer alone could not summon.

MY TEAM

My partner Mark Jankowski and I have built our consulting business first and foremost as a team.

Proof of the strength of a team, unfortunately, often comes during moments of adversity within your company. In late 2005, Mark's wife suffered a debilitating illness. Our entire team met to prepare ourselves for two goals: to support Mark and his family with the utmost competence and compassion, and to keep building the business in Mark's absence while he cared for his wife and children.

We applied the preparation principles to our challenge. We tried to help Mark steer through his personal challenges by making that our primary objective. I sought advice from a psychiatrist/business consultant to help our team understand how to support Mark and his family. We looked at alternative ways to structure the company and cover Mark's clients and responsibilities in his absence.

And devil's advocating with our other managers led to a strategy that won us a contract with Verizon. After overcoming the initial resistance to court Verizon without Mark, we decided to compete against other submissions in a proposal process. To make our proposal the best possible, we designated the most analytical people in our office to take the devil's advocate position regarding the submission. They helped us sharpen our submission and win a big contract despite the odds. We viewed Mark's absence as a rallying point and as a challenge to prepare even more diligently and methodically. We realized how well we had our own "next man up" system in place. Then our newest partner, Todd Lenhart, developed a script for the final Verizon presentation that allowed Mark to step in and play a major role in the final days of the deal.

Thereafter, Mark's return only took our team to another level. By using different colleagues to cover for Mark's responsibilities, we brought everyone's game to a new level. Obviously this is easier in a small company like the Shapiro Negotiations Institute. However, the same principle can be applied to divisions within larger companies.

CARL, LARRY, AND THE BATTLE OF THE BOATS ON THE JERSEY SHORE

When I was a teenager, I used to work at a boat rental shop called Carl's near Atlantic City. We rented fishing boats to summer vacationers. Our staff was the typical teenage hodgepodge that fills jobs at the beaches in the summer. And yet, for the owner of our business, this was his livelihood. We had summer jobs; he had a business on which he and his family depended for their livelihood. There always is a certain incompatibility in such situations. But Carl faced stiff competition from Larry's on the next pier for the day fishing business. So there was really no initial overlap between his project team—we dock boys—and his preparation team. He had no devil's advocate among us; we were merely looking for some summer money and enjoyed being around the water. Carl hoped for the best, counting on us to at least have a good work ethic and be team players.

The key to success in Carl's business was getting the boats out as quickly and as early as possible in the morning. This meant getting the bait, rods, gas cans, motors, and life preservers in order and checking all safety and weight requirements in as precise a manner as possible. At the beginning of my first summer we allocated a dock boy to each boat. A single boy was responsible for stocking each boat with everything that fishing and safety required. Larry's was kicking the, er, bait out of us. We couldn't figure out why. Carl grew more frustrated by the day.

But one morning Carl conferred with one of the older boys—probably his first devil's advocate among us—and heeded his advice to organize the team differently. He designated a bait boy, rod boy, fuel boy, life preserver boy, cleaning boy, et cetera, based on our proficiency with each task rather than assigning us each to a single boat.

Larry's business was next to us and had been around longer, but we started to soon beat him because people knew if they came to our pier they could get in and out more quickly. They could start fishing sooner in the morning and get home faster with their fish in the afternoon. We were not the perfect team—Carl obviously could have had better preparation partners. We were a bunch of kids and could offer Carl little advice on how to run his business. But by engaging one of us as his preparation partner, Carl reinvented his business. By putting the right people on his team into the right roles, he gained the competitive edge to start to beat Larry.

In this chapter, I profile three people dedicated to the art of picking a team and defining individual roles. Mark Shapiro, general manager of the Cleveland Indians, expects input, challenges, and questions from members at all levels of his team. Shari-Huene Johnson, a principal at an innovative school for challenged kids, maximizes the talents of each member of her staff. Andrew Klemmer, a manager of some of the most acclaimed building projects in the past twenty-five years, sequentially coordinates a diverse and far-flung group of the world's best contractors, architects, and engineers. These three people illustrate the benefits of preparing by paying inordinate attention to the way in which a team fits together.

THE PRECISE TEAM

Mark Shapiro

Mark Shapiro, my son, is a team player. He is a leader, a listener, and a competitor. Mark, as general manager of the Cleveland Indians since 2002, has innovatively picked and managed his front office team to keep a lower budget club competitive in a sport increasingly dominated by wealthy franchises. These traits earned him the Major League Executive of the Year Award in 2005 and helped the Indians achieve the American League Central title and tie for most wins in baseball in 2007. His ability to prepare by identifying his front office team members and allocating their responsibilities in a way that leverages their skills is a lesson for any business competing against others with richer resources.

From an early age, Mark found satisfaction in helping his siblings, in mediating peer problems, and in essentially eliminating nonsense from human interaction. He is a do-it-right kind of guy. And he realizes that his organization's success is tied to building a team of similarly committed collaborators and putting people in the roles most suited to their talents.

Mark's approach to his team can be broken down into four notable parts: (1) his emphasis on utilizing interns; (2) his embrace of information technology specialists; (3) his insistence on precision in communication; and (4) his recognition of the importance of a succession plan at every position. These parts drive a very effective whole: all levels of Mark's team interact with and inform each other in an insistent way.

"Because our business is a business where the assets—players—are human, our reality is that our assets are imperfect," Mark said. "This job is a quest to do everything possible to put systems in place to control all the things you can because with human assets there are so many variables. You want to sleep knowing you've done everything possible to put yourself in a position to succeed. And the best way to do this is by assembling as good a team as you can."

The unpredictability of human behavior and human performance, coupled with economic disparities among teams in Major League Baseball, means that competence and collaboration are essential to compete with financial Goliaths like the New York Yankees, Boston Red Sox, and Los Angeles Angels.

The daily task of Mark's front office team is to monitor and assess the baseball team they field in Cleveland, their farm teams, and the major- and minor-league talent of every other team in baseball. That complexity lies in the number of variables involved in such an evaluation: medical history, arm strength, hand-eye coordination, personality, character, leadership ability, reliability as a teammate, intelligence, and work ethic. And let's not forget bat speed and base-running skills.

So Mark's challenge, like that of any general manager in the league, is to build and maintain the front office team that monitors and assesses the risk, value, and talent on the team they field and the teams the Indians compete with.

He starts at the first rung with his interns. Mark spends almost as much energy and focus on hiring his interns as he does on signing up his draft picks.

"That's one of the most important details in my business,

believe it or not," Mark said. "It starts with the interns. Every single time we hire at that level we are looking for an impact person. As a culture we obsess about our entry-level hires. We do rigid interviews, thorough checks on references and background, test analytic thinking. And we look to create a track for succession and promotion."

The Indians receive literally hundreds of applications for their internships. A critical selection criterion is the applicants' response to a heavy-duty questionnaire. They are asked to write about topics like the "subjective evaluation vs. objective analysis in player procurement," "factors in making a selection in the amateur draft," and the "importance and valuation of closers."

Interns who have progressed through the Indians' system or who have moved on to bigger jobs elsewhere include Arizona Diamondbacks general manager Josh Byrnes, Pittsburgh Pirates GM Neal Huntington, and former LA Dodger GM Paul DePodesta.

Mark's second notable innovation is the prominence he gives to his software engineer in meetings and critical decisions. Baseball is still an old-fashioned, insular business. Change comes slowly and begrudgingly. Mark is at the forefront of the use of technology to improve the information gathered from evaluation and scouting.

One of Mark's early decisions was to better utilize a software engineer who developed and maintains the Indians' proprietary software called DiamondView. Lisa Fontenelli at Goldman Sachs used her team of analysts and software programmers to work together in assessing risk and value in much the same way that Mark's team at the Indians does. They are both focused on every moving part of the supply chain. In Lisa's case, it was manufactured goods; in Mark's world, it is the even more complex human capital that composes a professional sports organization.

"DiamondView is our own system that allows us to take all that information that we are constantly processing and access it quickly and efficiently," Mark said. "Matt Tagliaferri, our engineer, is always programming, always adjusting the system. In a sense we are all involved in the continual development and evolution of that system. There are not many guys like Matt in this business. The software allows us to take all the information that scouts, medical experts, coaches, and sports psychologists provide and synthesize it. The net result is that we spend less time gathering information and more time analyzing. This gives us the best chance to make an effective personnel decision."

This constant focus on synthesis is what so many management teams lack. Mark uses software to help achieve it. It forms a key part of his third "team" tenet—an insistence on precision in communication. So many teams are plagued by generalities in opinion, advice, and encouragement. Mark is constantly trying to defy this by forcing a shift from the habitual "rhetorical and emotional assessment" to "specific and precise feedback."

"The culture of precision that the Indians seek to create applies both to scouting and front office decision making as well as player development. In the past a staff member might say that a player 'just doesn't have it,'" Mark said. "That is a standard phrase in almost any business. We ask them to be more precise. Why? 'Because he has no command.' Why? 'Because his delivery is not consistent.' Why? 'Because he does not have a consistent release point.'

Ultimately we get to the root cause of the limitation, which then gives us the best chance to design an appropriate development plan."

This insistence on precision in communication could lead to tension in many organizations. Mark tries to eliminate this by focusing on selecting front office personnel whom he believes are not prone to defensiveness or self-centeredness.

"We are intolerant of insecurity and barriers on our team," Mark said. "We are just completely inflexible on that topic. That is the only thing, beside the variables on the field that we cannot control, which will undermine our ability to be successful. We demand respect and trust across every department at every level. Any amount of time or energy spent on anything other than mutual goals and common vision means someone else is already beating you."

This emphasis on security and trust is perhaps best illustrated by the Indians' openness about succession plans for each and every position. It is the fourth quality that defines the way Mark picks his team.

"Each and every one of my guys is charged with identifying and training his replacement internally," Mark said. "We are very open about this and meet about it. I have my successor, Chris Antonetti, in place just like everyone else."

That may sound like a funny way to run a business. Making turnover a primary focus of senior-level management may seem to some a poor use of time and energy.

But Mark sees it as a fundamental part of picking and maintaining a team, and his front office teammates whom I know view it as one of the major strengths of the operation.

It may be true that it is easier to build a team and play as a team in the business of team sports. It is what drew Mark to his job in the first place. But the stories of incompetence and internal strife are as legion in baseball as in any other business. A key to winning as a team or in any collective endeavor is where Mark finds his greatest satisfaction: preparing by using a front office with the right people in the right jobs built to work together in a creative, collaborative, and precise way.

PICKING THE DREAM TEAM

Shari Huene-Johnson

Often you can't hire a team. You inherit it. A leader who prepares by analyzing the abilities and experiences of team members can sometimes overcome amazing obstacles. We see that in what the team, led by principal Shari Huene-Johnson, accomplished at the William S. Baer School. Shari shows a special knack for assigning people to the task that best suits their talents and interests.

Shari had a jack-of-all-trades—known only as Mr. Lyles—as the backbone of her team. No first name; most wonder if he ever had one. He is the eighty-five-year-old custodian at the Baer School, an outpost for severely handicapped children and young adults from the wrong side of the socioeconomic tracks in Baltimore. It is a special school for special kids. Some kids are missing arms and legs; others suffer from an assortment of health conditions and mental challenges; many are some of the happiest people I have ever seen.

The Baer students seem to realize that Mr. Lyles and his

colleagues are helping them achieve a higher level of life experience than most outsiders would think conceivable.

Mr. Lyles is known to wear his white tuxedo and do song-and-dance routines for the kids. He is known to sit at the lunch counter and spoon-feed children who can't hold utensils. He had unique passion for kids and insight into their lives.

Passion and insight—Shari, now retired, picked her team based on these two criteria. Her method offers a lesson for education professionals and businesspeople alike. Shari wants a team with passion and insight so that she can delegate to them, learn from them, and, ultimately, keep her customers satisfied. Whether the customers are schoolkids or Fortune 500 companies, medical patients or legal clients, the story of Shari's team can be a model for anyone picking a team as part of their preparation.

"His age did not matter to me," Shari said. "Where can you find a custodian who will help feed children and can still clean rings around anyone I know in his business? There was no mandatory retirement age, so I kept him. He taught all of us how to work with the kids. He has this love for them. Your team has to share the common mission and you have to be able to learn from each other."

When Shari started as principal at the Baer School in 1989, she knew she needed to spend as much time working with teachers and students as she spent on administrative issues. She is a person who inspires, and her greatest contribution to the school would be helping teachers learn to teach better. So Shari needed to spend large parts of her days in the classroom. And to do this, she needed to assign tasks to teachers who could handle some of her administrative responsibilities.

She first studied the teachers on staff for their specific talents and personalities. Then Shari picked a core team by matching these talents and personalities with the core components of the complex administration of a unique school.

"My core covered all the needs with their specific skills," Shari said. "But they all also have that strong love for the kids." In other words, they brought the insight and passion that Shari used as her criteria.

Shari saw in William Van Arnam and Irene Stevens two people with a dedication to organization and structure. She made Van her records person. He tracks the health issues of kids on a daily basis, monitors their academic progress, and records attendance. In a place where health emergencies are a near-daily occurrence, he keeps all critical phone numbers for family and health-care providers. Irene tracks all special education records and orchestrates the regular parent days where over 85 percent of parents come to discuss the progress and challenges of their children.

Shari saw Edna Parker as a real innovator of a tricky curriculum. While reading, writing, and arithmetic are long-term goals for these students, more pressing instruction is needed in hygiene, basic tasks, and physical skills. Edna traveled the country learning about advances in this special curriculum, distilled those insights for the Baer School, and worked with teachers to implement them. Her special achievements included the addition of a swimming pool and an assortment of therapy and workout equipment to the school's educational infrastructure.

Shari saw Arlene Dorsey as a real spitfire who could literally get people to move. She was in charge of one of the most challenging issues for the Baer School: transportation. Most of the 250 students come to school on specially equipped buses. Private nurses, oxygen tanks, and wheelchairs often tag along for the ride. Arlene would have been a great head of a NASCAR team in the pit—she simply loves to make things move.

Shari saw in Anton Scott a guy who loves a party. So she made him and his lively personality the head of special events. The goal at Baer is to make the students' lives as normal as possible, so proms, field trips, and even regular academic testing are part of the plan. Anton even makes testing days fun.

For health care, head nurse Barbara Kadin combines kindness toward the kids with an insider's knowledge of how the health department, doctors' offices, and even insurance companies work.

"You have to really visualize not only your goals but your team and how together you will work toward those goals," Shari said. "In selecting the team to meet a challenge, you have to find people who not only share your vision but who add to it. My team kept adding to my vision. We would meet regularly and I would walk away with new ideas and energy from each of them."

All of this preparation required funds to translate into execution. Shari realized she could not implement all her team's new ideas and finance their programs without a supplementary budget. Baer is a public school with the same budgetary constraints of any other school but with larger budgetary issues. So Shari picked another team for external fund-raising. People from throughout the community were asked to join the Baer Partnership Board and raised funds for the pool, computers, new equipment, repairs, and even secured a grant from the USGA Foundation to build a handicapped golf course behind the building! She used the same criteria—passion and insight—for assembling this team. She keeps it simple, and her teams succeed.

Nearly two years after Shari's departure, her same team continues to serve the new principal. They all promised to do so for one year and now have stayed for two. Shari even helped lay out the succession plan that has kept the continuity of Baer.

All this preparation and attention to assigning roles to her team members' passion and insight served Shari's singular goal: keeping your customers satisfied.

A TRANSPARENT TEAM

Andy Klemmer

You build a building piece by piece. Likewise, the methodical construction of your team leads to a great building.

In the world of construction manager Andy Klemmer, you designate a team piece by piece and draw on each new member's wisdom and experience to inform the next hire. Andy's gentle demeanor masks a strong will: with the support of a building's owners, he insists on finding architects, engineers, and other professionals in his network who best suit the particular demands of buildings from Miami to Manhattan, from Bilbao, Spain, to San Francisco.

That's what helped make the Glass Pavilion at the Toledo

Museum of Art (TMA) worthy of what *New York Times* architecture critic Nicolai Ouroussoff wrote in 2006: "Once you drift outside again, the tree branches seem to sway more gently, the light feels softer, the world more tender. Most important, you are more attuned to the distances between people. There are few higher compliments you could pay a building." Or pay to a team.

Project teams are a funny bunch: egos, incompetence, and greed can overwhelm the noblest architectural under-takings. Picking your team in this business is as important as coaches assembling their staff or players. It requires the balancing of talent and teamwork, experience and open-ness, singularity of purpose and willingness to collaborate.

TMA hired Andy Klemmer's Paratus Group in 2001 to manage the development of the Pavilion. They did them-selves—and architecture—a favor by letting Andy use his criteria to assemble the project team. The design by Japa-nese architects Kazuyo Sejima and Ryue Nishizawa of the firm SANAA inspired Ouroussoff's praise. But highly sequenced selection and preparation of the entire project team is equally responsible for Toledo's new gem.

"The building is a result of not just executing a design but of the entire team contributing to the design," Andy said. "By learning from each other we built a better building. The team synthesized information from every design consultant, the structural engineer, the façade consultant, the cost esti-mator, the mechanical engineer, and the other specialists. The selection process and the timing of their joining the team rarely happen as purely as it did in Toledo."

The personality of the players is important to Andy when

he chooses a team. But precision and technical proficiency come first. When he can blend all three, the result is an achievement like the Morgan Library in New York or the Glass Pavilion.

"Toledo is historically very good at being at the front end of an architect's celebrity," Andy said. "They found the firm SANAA, and, even though they were less known than many other potential architects, they really fit the needs of the collection and institution. Certainly they had something of that quiet Japanese elegance and artistry that really resonated with the glass collection."

And so, with SANAA onboard, TMA and Andy established a process for growing the team by using each member hired to help pick each subsequent addition to the team. The museum, SANAA, and Paratus selected the executive architect to oversee the project and interact with the city during construction. Then, with the executive architect's input, they selected the mechanical and structural consultants. Then, with those consultants joining the selection process, the team selected a cost consultant. And on and on.

The executive architect had to be on the ground and execute the complex design. "Roger Berkowitz, Toledo's director, really understood that this thing required a sophistication on the execution side that matched the design side," Andy said. "The position of executive architect could not be a consolation prize for a local firm. There are two critical qualities that an executive architect needs. They have to be egoless and technically precise. They have to dedicate themselves completely to someone else's design and then produce documents based on that design that are incredibly precise.

And they have to know the building code—and know how to go around, under, or over it to get the design approved."

After interviewing numerous firms from around the country, the group selected Kendall Heaton from Houston, Texas. They came onboard and immediately mastered the local code issues and paid repeated visits to the building department to keep them apprised of the plans as they developed.

The team next worked through the back and forth of building design. SANAA produced a building model that fit the aesthetic and practical needs of the museum. During this design period, Andy turned his attention to the engineers.

"You don't want the engineers getting too detailed too early," Andy said. "The design needs a little time to develop without the burden of detailed engineering. At the same time, you cannot wait too long if you want the engineering to inform the design and you want to know that the design supports the critical functions of the building operationally."

In this case the engineering informed the design very closely. The size of the glass pieces were dictated by oven sizes in China as reported by Front Design, the façade consultant selected by the team.

"Think about it—how wide, how tall, how much the pieces of glass could be bent," Andy said. "We knew we had to select a façade consultant early given the primacy of glass in the early designs. We needed to find someone who was not set in their ways, someone who saw their job as enabling the design, not restricting it. And Front stretched the design by finding bigger glass than they knew existed!"

The next hire was the cost estimator. The museum, despite its selection of avant-garde architects, is a fiscally conservative institution with budget constraints. For this selection, Paratus suggested the leading cost consultants from New York and Chicago. The team selected a firm together.

"If only the owner hires the cost consultant, that firm will forever be known as the owner's cost consultant," Andy said. "Everyone will just think that these are the owner's numbers and nothing more. But if you include the architect and engineers in the decision, the cost consultant becomes the team's selection. It gives the cost consultant a real credibility and builds support for him in doing battle with the contractor on pricing."

The contractor comes last for Andy.

"The contractor comes last because that is where all the money goes," Andy said with a laugh. "Getting them too early is a problem for two reasons. First they can kill a design. Second, they can lose their incentive to price the project well so that they get and keep the job. There is always another price or a better price they can go out and get, but they need an incentive to hustle. If they have the job and their fee is guaranteed, what is the incentive to work hard? But getting them too late brings them into the documents too late to have the documents improved by their involvement."

For Andy, as it should be for anyone involved in any complicated project, preparing by assigning the right team member from his deep bench of accomplished players is the cornerstone of a great project.

KEY POINTS

TEAM

- A key to preparing with a team is putting the right people in the right roles. You know their skills and match them with appropriate parts of the game plan.

- Team members also play a key part in preparation— helping you define objectives, ponder precedents, and set strategy.

- As you work through scripting, the final principle, good team members support you with devil's advocacy and the opportunity to rehearse your script.

- Mark Shapiro knows the skills of his team members inside out. He faces a hundred topics on any given day and invariably prepares with the teammate who is best suited to help him on each one.

- Shari Huene-Johnson is a master at delegating responsibilities to the team member who most excels in the challenge at hand. She maximizes both their talents and their production.

- Andy Klemmer shows how to build a team, step by step, in a sequence that builds the momentum and improves the cost effectiveness of a construction project.

10

WHAT YOU SAY AND HOW YOU SAY IT

Write the Script

What is the greatest movie script ever written? Obviously, there is no single answer. But many screenwriters would cite one of my favorites—Robert Towne's *Chinatown*. The script is recognized as a virtuoso performance at the height of what may have been a second golden age of Hollywood artistry. Its script weaves a film noir involving the exposure of a seamy family history into a political and socioeconomic backdrop. The result is a gripping and deliciously sordid story. Then there are the scenes: Jack Nicholson getting his nose sliced; John Huston looking into the bulging eye of a dead fish; the phone ringing and Faye Dunaway's face showing pure dread.

I see the script for *Chinatown* as the summation of a rigid preparation of the story by Towne. He deploys just about every major aspect of an actual fraudulent water crisis perpetrated upon California and its voters as the backdrop for a story of a family's own corruption. The script brings together, about as well as any American screenplay ever has, the personal and the political.

So, movie maniac that I am, I try to emulate the thoroughness but by no means the length of *Chinatown* when I write my scripts for my business activities. Without great delivery by actors, great lines in a script fall flat. Scripts give me and the people I advise confidence in what we express and how we express it; otherwise, the other side can sense a lack of confidence.

You cannot predict the actual course of legislative testimony, a sales pitch, a steroids investigation, or a board presentation. But you can rehearse the scenarios you anticipate. By thinking through and writing down scripts for the way you think events will unfold, you will have a solid foundation for dealing with the twists and turns of actual events. Frequently when I prepare a script, I bracket scenarios and statements that the script itself may not directly address but that I want to at least have thought about prior to a meeting or presentation. A script can't address all possibilities, but it can prepare you for most. I also have a colleague review my script and be a devil's advocate with me to help raise the effectiveness of its content and delivery.

Yes, writing a script takes time, but not as much as you might think, and it will prepare you for something you'll come across at least 75 percent of the time. Pretty good odds, so no time wasted. I script—write out in shorthand—what I want to express.

People from all sorts of professions—lawyers, CEOs, top doctors—repeatedly shock me. You often come across someone who strikes you as so accomplished and refined when you first meet him that you assume he is the best deal maker or project manager or musician or doctor imaginable. But what is surprising is how many times I see these types of people fail once they have to engage the other side or audience. What they said they were going to do and what they did in the speech or the meeting seemed to change for the worse once they were in the glare of a transaction and felt the other side's potential resistance.

For example, I have observed people in a negotiation go into a meeting having stated a clear intention to make a tough demand—say, an "ask" of $1 million per year for rights to comarket with their product. Yet when the pressure of a face-to-face negotiation and the fear of potential rejection arises, their conviction starts to waver. What they articulate is "something in the range of $1 million" or between "$750,000 and $1,000,000"—in either case, they have already put themselves below their projected ask.

Public speakers can really benefit from scripting, too. People I know tell me they think I am a good extemporaneous speaker. Secretly I chuckle. While I want people to feel that the presentation—keynote, seminar, toast, or roast—is extemporaneous, the reality is that I have scripted out my presentation, had it reviewed by an associate (my teammate), and have prepared it (though I will not read it). I prepare to come across as extemporaneous. The script preparation process not only helps me build confidence, but also enables me to bone up on or get new insights into issues I may have insufficiently understood. The simple act of writing it down shows what you really know or don't know. Writing a script helps you confront whether or not you are "BSing."

I follow this same process in difficult negotiations where I have to make a demand that might make me feel uncomfortable. By scripting out my questions and potential responses from the other person beforehand, I prepare myself to *not* show discomfort or uncertainty that comes with a "tough ask."

For example, when you are involved in the give-and-take of a negotiation in professional sports, you sometimes seek huge amounts of money for your clients. And as some superstars hit their late twenties, you have to ask their original team, sometimes one of the less wealthy franchises, to pay an amount that it might struggle to afford. A certain discomfort arises that could undermine your confidence when you make an ask that exceeds what you know will be acceptable to the other side. Practicing with a script before making a proposal can build your confidence level so that the tough ask comes off without a blink or stutter.

Even when the situation is not as intense as a big contract negotiation, scripting what you want to communicate helps you develop a comfort level with expressing the reason for your position on difficult issues. And this can apply to personal interactions like breaking difficult news to a spouse or sibling as much as to business deals.

In most cases, I don't write a script word for word, but use bullet points and simply try to sketch out the main pieces of my presentation. I use brackets where I sense potential uncertainty so I can try to make an audible change like good quarterbacks change the play at the line of scrimmage. I write phrases like "ask why" or "probe here" in the margins at critical points in the script. Good devil's advocates will point out those moments by putting themselves in the shoes of your client or counterpart.

Scripting can feel forced or mechanical. But what may start out as a cumbersome exercise can become an especially gratifying one if it involves a good team member. Scripting is the last step on the Preparation Principles Checklist because it is the culmination of all the preparation that you have done.

KIRBY PUCKETT'S SCRIPT

Somewhere at the midpoint of my career—rather late in the game—I fully grasped the importance of scripting. My sports agentry business requires me to make lots of asks, or demands, that are substantially higher than what the other side—team ownership—is willing to accept. Although I sometimes found myself uncomfortable with the process of overasking, I realized that I should question just as vigorously the practice of underoffering by the team.

I wanted to strengthen the expression of that ask. I decided that I needed to overcome my doubts and make more powerful proposals. In sports negotiations there is frequently a major gap that exists between the sides. Aiming high or low, depending on which side you are on, is a part of the process.

In 1992, I scripted the negotiation for Kirby Puckett's

then significant $32 million, five-year contract. To make the high ask that led to it—in order to get comfortable and confident with it—I decided to script out the negotiation with Michael Maas, my partner in the sports firm. Michael proved a perfect devil's advocate. Just as a good acting coach helps an actor learn and say her lines, Michael and I scripted the negotiation—from content to delivery. We literally conducted rehearsals, or mock debates, and played parts. This collaboration instilled confidence in the initial ask I would make on Kirby's behalf.

I remember sketching out on a yellow legal pad the rationale for this ask. I prepared myself to deliver to Minnesota Twins general manager Andy McPhail: "Andy, a $36 million contract is entirely reasonable for Kirby in light of the fact that we had every indication from both the Phillies and the Red Sox that they would offer Kirby at least that much. Last summer we were willing to take significantly less, but the club rejected that proposal, and it is only fair that the market help determine the appropriate compensation level for Kirby. We hope that you see the wisdom of making a deal like that to keep him off the market."

I confidently made my demand, and as a result achieved more than Kirby's goal. He became one of the highest-paid players in Major League Baseball at the time even though he played on a small-market team.

It is important to remember in negotiations that much is lost for the want of asking. This is based on an old English proverb, and I love it. Much is lost for the want of asking, and much is lost for the want of scripting. And you get more comfortable with asking by scripting.

WHY CAN'T YOU LEARN YOUR LINES?

Scripting can also be fun; you can treat it a bit like a puzzle and later compare how well you put the pieces together.

Yet, of all the preparation principles, I find that clients and students resist this one the most—even more than doing timelines. It does not come naturally. It may feel the most burdensome. That is because people forget to keep it fun. My imagination of movie scenes does this for me.

You may recall that in the introduction to this book I discussed my belief in the idea of professional cross-training. The analogy ran like this: a track star or basketball player can enhance his or her performance by dedicating training time to swimming or biking. Such hybrid training is an acknowledged and much-used technique to take performance to a higher level. Studying how others script can provide the breakthrough you need. I believe that this concept of cross-training applies as a part of preparation for almost any profession.

So whatever your profession, pay special attention to the three profiles in this chapter. Dr. Ray DePaulo, head of the department of psychiatry at Johns Hopkins Hospital, uses scripts to prepare for everything from budget presentations to patient communications. Trial lawyer Paul Sandler uses the litigators in his department to be devil's advocates for the arguments he scripts. Seattle Supersonics general manager Sam Presti makes scripting an integral part of contract and trade talks in order to reduce the pressure of face-to-face negotiations. These three preparers' benefits are confidence and the nimbleness to adjust to unforeseen events.

THE SCRIPT DOCTOR

Dr. Ray DePaulo

Dr. Ray DePaulo, an expert on the ups and downs of manic depression, is almost manic about scripting. While you wait outside his office door at Johns Hopkins Hospital, you can hear him excitedly talking about the upcoming hospital budget meeting. Ray is the chair of Hopkins's Department of Psychiatry, one of the best in the world. And, from what you can overhear, it seems that managing the Department of Psychiatry is a lot like managing a division at a company. There are budget battles, turf wars, and personnel struggles.

Ray works his way through it all and finds time to remain a world-class psychiatrist by relying on scripting for most of his encounters and negotiations. One day as Greg and I sat outside his office, we eavesdropped as Ray rehearsed his script. You could hear him pacing the floor; he stops to discuss suggestions from his devil's advocates; he adjusts his voice's emphasis like an actor learning his lines.

Ray and members of his faculty of 170 psychiatrists and psychologists script for most major presentations and negotiations, for grant interviews, and even for patient sessions. These highly intelligent people don't rely on their smarts; they take the time to script. When I feel too rushed to script, I draw inspiration from this crowd. They tend to make you believe in what you teach. They motivate you to script.

"I would say I spend 40 percent of my day preparing," Ray said. "And of that 40 percent scripting occupies the largest single part of it. It is essential to always go back and script even for a meeting you feel you have already had before or for people you meet with regularly. I like how it makes me feel going into an event; and I like how it makes me look to my colleagues in terms of being prepared."

Ray was up until 12:30 the night before working on his script for this rehearsal that I listened in on. He is dealing with the threat of the transfer of a small portion of his annual budget—tied to a staff position that overlaps specialties—from his department back to the general budget for the Department of Medicine. It seems to be not so much a turf war as a vestige of the still uncomfortable coexistence between psychiatry and medicine in general.

You can imagine the stakes and the competition for resources at one of the top hospitals in the world that also happens to overlap with one of the top medical schools in the world. Not only do Ray and his department head peers face the normal budgetary tug-of-war that define any such entity; they also are highly competitive achievers at the pinnacle of their game.

"I love treating patients," Ray said. "But I accept and embrace the administrative stuff because I believe so much in what we are doing here. We need someone who understands the mission to be central to the needed administrative changes. So I try to prepare as thoroughly as I can for business tasks and for negotiations. But you need to harness your motivation with a system. I literally photocopy the preparation principles [Ray had participated in one of our seminars early in his chairmanship] and follow them step-by-step."

The method is what gives power and effectiveness to Ray's motivation. For this specific budget negotiation, he has a script on his desk that has Ray's statements filled in on the following outline:

1. Listen, ask questions, clarify answers; discuss new ideas—short-, intermediate-, and long-term goals of Johns Hopkins Medicine.

   a. Short-term

   b. Intermediate-term

   c. Long-term

2. What does Medicine want that is distinct from our wants, the employees' wants?

3. Consequence: does the other department know that they are asking to take on a losing budget?

4. Consequences for the School of Medicine if even one of psychiatry's experts leave for another university: millions of dollars in research grants.

5. Alternatives: ask the hospital to take over the budget for a year, so decision makers will see what money is spent for and who should manage it.

6. Alternatives: support a more ambitious plan to integrate these programs across all Hopkins hospitals and campuses. This would reframe the current focus on psychiatry.

In the first half of his script, Ray is trying to bring everyone at the table to a common ground. Perhaps their collective analysis of short-, intermediate-, and long-term goals will spark the realization of some common ground. And Ray is also studying his counterparts—defining their interests. In this case, the inclusion of it in his script allows Ray to probe their motivations and examine how the issue at hand intersects with their own timeline. This may allow Ray to reposition his argument or propose a temporary solution that takes into account collective long-term goals.

In the second half of his script, Ray compares the other department's interests with those of his own department. Then he brainstorms ideas or solutions that can be win-wins. His emphasis on consequences is important, too. Sometimes you can point out consequences that affect the other side that they have not even realized. I know for a fact that Ray has done that in this negotiation, and it has significantly influenced the outcome of the negotiation.

"Unless I make myself write out the planner and the script, I never fully probe my situation, let alone the other side's," Ray said. "And it becomes a challenge like a competitive game. You can have fun with it."

The fun for Ray obviously comes when he gets to rehearse. Ray is a people person; he loves to talk and interact. You might expect stuffiness and isolation in the top of academia's ivory tower. But you have to remember what Ray said earlier—that he wants to be treating patients. Subconsciously or not, he transforms that impulse to want to interact with people into a real strength of his scripting.

"Again, I literally print out a list of the preparation principles and write answers to the questions," Ray said. "What are my objectives? What are their interests? Whose career are we helping or hurting? Whose budget? What are the short-, intermediate-, and long-term goals? Then I look for precedents—for example, where else do PhDs rather than MDs really run clinical programs? How have they done? What are the management alternatives? What are the deadlines? Then I bring in my crack team—psychiatrists, psychologists, researchers, administrative people—and I tell them to grill me."

That grilling—as much by e-mail as behind closed doors—is extraordinary. I have seen it. It is like what I imagine the top preparation for a presidential debate must be like. Ray's people role-play; they ask him questions he had not thought of, they make demands, and they even play-act rudeness and aggression with him. He leaves the room bedraggled but more prepared than the other guy. So many of the preparation principles intersect in Hopkins's Department of Psychiatry—precedents, pick your team, do a timeline, and so on. But they demonstrate that you can use one principle as the pivot for all the others. In Ray's case, it is scripting.

And it is especially pleasing to know that he applies scripting to his treatment of patients, too. Ray and his people see some of the most difficult psychiatric cases from around the world. They see the world's princes and the poorest people from rough neighborhoods in Baltimore. In my role as chair of his advisory board, I was privileged to learn about the inner workings and techniques of psychiatric treatment, and it is one of the joys of my professional career to know that Ray to a large degree incorporates the preparation principles into his most important work: saving and improving lives.

"The biggest challenge we face is when a patient is acutely ill," Ray said. "This is really a disorder of the brain that makes it hard for a person to reason objectively and accurately. Also depression imposes a real negative bias. So I often start with a template—Hamlet's soliloquy. To be or not to be. I follow Hamlet's script but adjust my lines to the case. This is simplistic because there are numerous therapeutic techniques involved but the basic script with tailored lines works. And delivery is important, too. So I rehearse that."

Ray's Hamlet speech, however, always ends with a different sort of life-affirming poetry. His preparation with so many patients and even some failures, "losses" as he lamentably calls them, has helped him hone the conclusion of his soliloquy.

"I had a recent session with a woman whom I have been treating for severe depression for fifteen years," Ray said. "We have not been able to solve the problem, a brain disorder, with medication or therapy. But we have helped her adjust to a reasonably satisfying and functional life. Recently she's been depressed again, and I brought out a script that I had been rehearsing for a long time for her. I told her that the staff and nurses had for a long time considered her a heroine for living her life in the face of depression. She was moving her life in the correct direction despite carrying a three-hundred-pound gorilla on her shoulders. I told her she is amazing, just remarkable, a person of real value."

Whether scripting to save jobs in his department or scripting to save the lives of his patients, Ray scripts with a devotion to preparation that can stave off three-hundred-pound gorillas.

REHEARSING YOUR SCRIPT

 *Paul Sandler*

Paul Sandler knows how to play the blues. His harmonica shakes and shines as he blows out an old Muddy Waters tune. Paul is also one of the top trial lawyers in the country who a few years ago won the high-profile Hillary Clinton Hollywood fund-raising case. And when he delivers an opening or closing argument in court, he becomes the same man in motion who plays the harmonica. He loses himself; he moves and gestures like a man from another world.

The key to his success and apparent spontaneity: rehearsing a script and letting others critique his performance as part of his preparation.

Paul is always looking for linkages across everything from his profession to his pastime. And in blues harmonica he sees an apt metaphor for trial lawyering.

"Playing the harmonica or any musical instrument well is all about practicing," Paul said. "But practicing in the wrong way can do more damage than not practicing at all. You could be practicing in the wrong key and therefore not practicing the correct music even though you think you are. You could be practicing the wrong technique. Like a golfer who keeps swinging and swinging, you are incorporating your mistakes into your performance. You are actually practicing your mistakes."

That's why Paul's harmonica teacher plays devil's advocate as Paul practices.

Paul has a methodical manner of preparing for his trials,

and he has built a reputation on being the best-prepared guy in the courtroom. In his case, scripting involves writing and rehearsing scenarios, and it also involves a level of mental preparation akin to the focus he needs to play the harmonica well.

"Preparation is an indispensable quality for me as a trial lawyer," Paul said. "One reason I became a trial lawyer is because you don't have to be brilliant to excel. You just have to be well prepared. I have seen the most articulate lawyers left with unthinkably poor results when their opposing parties were better prepared."

Paul is a bit of an amateur historian, too, and he particularly loves to use Abraham Lincoln as a role model for being a trial lawyer. Because of his prominence and accomplishments in history, Lincoln's impressive career as a trial lawyer is sometimes forgotten. Lincoln once remarked that "in order to win in court you need to know the other side's case better than they do."

The first step in Paul's system is debriefing clients and witnesses as thoroughly as possible. As preparation, Paul spends a lot of time putting himself in the shoes and inside the head of the person whom he will be interviewing. This is what great reporters like Liane Hansen (see pages 146–50) do as they get ready to interview people for their stories.

Paul then builds a master chronology of events and backs it up with supporting documents. He writes out the chronology and builds a filing system to match it. He does this for two reasons. First, the preparation informs his ultimate scripting. Second, this kind of tangible layout gives Paul a confidence that you might equate with reading sheet music. He sees the case in front of him; he visualizes it. This preparation turns the facts into the notes that become the substance of his trial performance.

It is also at this point that Paul feels a theme or theory of the case start to cohere.

"The theme is the spinal cord of the case if you will," Paul said. "It has to focus on the listener. My work is receiver centered. You have to realize in this business, as in most any other, that you are not the most important aspect of the communications cycle. The listener is. The theme has to embrace the listener."

With this chronology in hand, Paul feels prepared to do what he calls point-counterpoint.

"I need to study the other side's view and learn their case after I feel I have mastered mine," Paul said. "This is where Lincoln comes in. This is an evolving process, but you end up discovering different points of view or strategies from the other side and then adjusting your own."

After Paul has prepared his case and studied the other side, he then turns to the applicable law to superimpose a framework on the case. By now he has his script structured and filled in. He is ready to practice it enough so that it becomes instinctual. Appearing scripted in a courtroom or in a presentation is the last thing an attorney wants. You know when you are doing it—you feel mechanical and self-conscious. Paul makes his presentation seem spontaneous by rehearsing his script with devil's advocates. Although his case is scripted, it doesn't appear so because he has rehearsed it so many times with teammates.

He even hires jury consultants to listen to his presentation; he does mock court sessions with other attorneys; he makes his wife suffer through his rehearsals; and when there is no one left, he turns to his loyal dog as his last-standing audience member.

Paul recalls one major case in which he was convinced that a witness had lied before a grand jury about having had an affair with his client. But he knew from his preparation for the case that delving into personal lives could turn off some juries very quickly.

"In a mock trial I decided to see how cross-examining the witness might come across," Paul said. "My mock jurors reacted very harshly against me when I probed her personal life, and actually doing so in court might have cost me the case." This sort of scripting with devil's advocates is less common in legal preparation than one might think. There are some incredibly talented and articulate lawyers, but many of them fall back solely on their brimming self-confidence, which allows master preparers like Paul to sneak in and grab a victory.

Paul also learns from scripting that a compelling fact is not necessarily a pertinent one.

"Every juicy fact does not necessarily advance your theme," Paul said. "The key is to keep your focus on your theme. Keep advancing it. That is how you keep the key party in the communication interaction, the jury, focused."

The lesson here transcends trial lawyering. Any presentation or negotiation requires this disciplined approach to maintaining the theme or narrative.

Scripting for Paul is a process of marshalling the facts, developing a theme, rehearsing his presentation with devil's advocates, and then rehearsing some more. In the balance between preparation and instinct, you can almost see the moment in Paul's method where preparation blends into action. And yet you will never see him rely on instinct too soon even though he has been winning cases for over thirty years. He keeps preparing today like he did in his early days. In fact, I bet he is as proud of having become a master script writer as an accomplished trial lawyer.

SCRIPTING CHAMPIONSHIP SEASONS

 *Sam Presti*

Sam Presti became assistant general manager of the San Antonio Spurs at the tender age of twenty-eight. Then in 2007, at the age of thirty, he took over the Seattle Supersonics, becoming the youngest general manager in the NBA.

While he was at the Spurs he developed his scripting abilities by collaborating with the team's legendary general manager, R. C. Buford, as they prepared for contract negotiations with star players such as Manu Ginobili and Tony Parker. The scripts gave the Spurs' management team the confidence to make strategic offers, reject demands, articulate alternative contract structures, and control the rhythm of a negotiation session. By writing, reviewing, and revising their scripts until the whole management team was satisfied, the Spurs came up with proposals that their designated negotiator could confidently express.

Sam learned old-school preparation from his grandfather, the most prepared person he has ever known. His grandfather's theory was that if the task or conversation is going to affect other people in any significant way, then you have an obligation to prepare for it in a way that goes beyond your comfort level.

"I think you owe it to your boss or anyone who cuts your check to prepare methodically," Sam said. "Because the method of scripting is the best way to ensure that you don't miss anything important or take any missteps, I have to look at it as an obligatory part of performing my job for the people I work for and with."

That to me is a striking thought. Disregarding whether you think you need to script, you still should do one because it is your obligation as a professional employee. The fact that companies do not make a certain preparation method obligatory is understandable; it may cut off creativity, box someone in, or even lead to mutiny. But it is impressive to me when an employee sees it as his or her obligation to prepare in a certain way. When I know that an employee of mine views preparation in this way, I know I have a winner on my hands.

Sam revises and improves his scripts like a basketball player repeats practicing a seventeen-foot jump shot when his or her comfort range is only fifteen feet.

"I recently read an essay on 'deliberate practice'," Sam said, "about enjoying the process, not just a good outcome but also the preparation leading up to it. It keeps you steady if things don't work out. If your self-validation can come completely out of the preparation process, then you can walk away from a win or a loss and still get satisfaction from your work."

The most important and practical reason Sam scripts is that it improves his presentations and leads to better agreements for both sides on a project or negotiation.

"My feeling when I first started scripting regularly was that the process was more about understanding the other person's strategies and points of view than your own," Sam said. "But the more I did it, the more I realized it was about finding my voice and gaining confidence in my own strategy and presentation. It is really about communicating your message and not getting off track or allowing emotions to trip you up. Scripting ensures clarity of direction but, more importantly, of presentation."

Here's a hypothetical scenario that Sam developed to illustrate the value of scripting, especially when it involves the nitty-gritty of contract negotiations.

Let's say Sam is going to meet with an agent about bringing a player to training camp. Normally the team does not offer compensation in such situations. Sam has found a small amount of funds available to give the player something, but knows he has to start low to manage their expectations. He prepares a script to get comfortable delivering the hard news to the agent, as well as for possible additional scenarios.

"We really would like to have Player X join us in camp. This would be a great opportunity for him to show what he can do and for our coaches to assess his fit with our team."

[Whether or not agent asks for compensation, add:]

"Based on our prior conversations, I feel good about our providing the kind of on-court opportunity you and X desire. Nevertheless, I can't offer you a compensation package, but you and X should carefully weigh what this opportunity means for him."

[If agent does not yield on the compensation point and in fact demands, for example, $100,000, Then:]

"*Hypothetically speaking if I can find $15,000 to add to your per diem, will that make a difference?*"

[If agent unwilling, then make final move in subsequent phone call:]

"*There is something we did once before, which I will try and get approval on if you get agreement from your client. We would raise our offer to $20,000 and if X is still on our roster 12 months from now we will pay him the additional $80,000. Let me know if this will work. If not, it's best that we both go in a different direction.*"

[In a similar case, the agent let Sam know that it would work.]

Sam constructs open-ended questions to probe the agent. He tries to foresee responses beforehand by adding the "if" parentheticals. He reminds himself to not act rashly and wait to make a more aggressive move in a subsequent phone call. He uses hypotheticals and precedents to persuade the agent. You get a sense of how Sam not only rehearses his lines but also leaves room for creative responses. He tries to build his predictions of the agent's behavior and strategy into the script, too.

Sam's scripts with the Spurs were collaborations inside an organization that is exemplary in the NBA for its management of the salary cap, identification of talent, and cohesiveness both on the court and in the front office. Sam had some great preparation mentors at the Spurs. I am sure his management team in Seattle will see more scripts than a studio in Hollywood. The scripting upstairs in the offices will match the repetition of the seventeen-foot jumpers that the best-prepared players will be practicing repeatedly on the court.

KEY POINTS

SCRIPT

- A script, properly devil's advocated, helps maximize the effectiveness of presentations, proposals, and especially "hard asks."

- When you write and practice your script, you rehearse word choice, tone, use of persuasive precedents, probing, and even silence.

- You can use scripts to flesh out ideas or approaches, discover new strategies or alternatives, or even realize something new about the other side's interests. Your devil's advocate helps you see the strengths and weaknesses in your script and helps you build your confidence.

- Ray DePaulo scripts for budget meetings and patient consultations alike: the fact that the head of the Department of Psychiatry at Johns Hopkins Hospital finds such value in scripting shows the usefulness of scripts in any field.

- Paul Sandler competes against some of the best trial lawyers in the country, and his incessant scripting with devil's advocates helps him win tough cases because his arguments are so honed and persuasive.

- Sam Presti learned contract negotiations as a member of the legendary San Antonio Spurs front office. Scripting dominates their management culture, and Sam's use of long, movie-like scripts or even shorthand notes has helped him become a strong negotiator.

11

THE CONSTANT PREPARER

Adjust and Learn from Mistakes

Preparation and adherence to the principles doesn't necessarily make perfect. Why? Because we are all destined to make mistakes. You can follow the principles diligently, but mistakes are as inevitable as daybreak or nightfall. The best preparers, however, learn from their errors and further prepare by using their insights to adjust either in midcourse or for the next challenge. Use of the principles doesn't end once the task begins. They continue to serve you when an error or unforeseen circumstance forces you to adjust your course. You re-prepare at such moments, and, by maintaining a systematic approach, you regroup more quickly and effectively.

I am the author of two other books, and people sometimes say to me, "Wow, it must be great to have accomplished enough that you are able to write books." That's certainly flattering, but I see it another way. I've made enough mistakes in my life to be able to learn from them and provide two books' worth of insights to readers so they can be effective when faced with similar issues and problems.

Like many people, I can let my emotions get the better of me and give myself the momentary satisfaction of telling off someone who is pushing my buttons. I've learned over the years that when you're in a confrontational situation, you are usually far better off thinking to yourself: "Hold your tongue. If you want to tell him to go to hell, you can do it just as well tomorrow as today." But I learned the lesson the hard way. For example, I once represented a celebrity and helped him get his personal and financial affairs in order. On one issue he refused to pay me what I believed was appropriate compensation. I got angry. I told him that I thought he was ungrateful and shortsighted, though my actual words were a bit less elegant.

I overreacted. He threatened litigation, resulting in greater anger on my part. It even cost me money. This was a defining moment, for it made me realize that emotional reactions signify a lack of control and that preparing my emotions fosters control. So I started to treat managing my emotions as a task: I prepared them methodically. I now prepare not only for the mechanics of the transaction itself—such as the deal points I want to achieve in a negotiation—but also psychologically so that my emotions don't undermine me. The two, the mechanics and the emotions, go hand in hand for me.

I now use a two-step process for controlling my emotions. First, I do something physical, such as putting a finger on my lip or practicing the old Thomas Jefferson method of counting under my breath. Second, that physical manifestation or trigger starts me down a psychological path that causes me to say to myself each time that I am not going to take this personally and I am not going to get personal. That little two-step process that I developed after years of emotional mistakes has allowed me to stay more true to my objectives and strategy.

I'm proud of another adjustment I made regarding the way in which my partner Mark Jankowski and I facilitate our seminars at the Shapiro Negotiations Institute. In our early years of partnership, we frequently led programs together and often were able to seamlessly hand off our presentation from one to the other in media res. It made me think of the best track relay teams beating records because of their dexterity in passing the baton.

We looked smooth in public, but acted like Felix and Oscar of *The Odd Couple* behind the scenes. For one of our first big presentations to a New York client, I forgot my tie and Mark forgot his dress pants. I wanted to map things out weeks in advance. Mark wanted to meet in the hotel room the night before to make sure that the pieces were all in place. I felt that my way was the right way. It's all about preparation, I would say. But Mark naturally enough thought the opposite: we would be equally prepared and more spontaneous if we rehearsed the night before and not weeks before. By my standards then, I felt Mark underprepared, or at least that he did too much last-minute rehearsing.

I suppose you could say we both learned from the mistake of being adamant about our respective approaches. Now when we teach together, we rehearse a few days in advance and not weeks ahead of time or the night before. Our programs still appear seamless, but our satisfaction in working together has grown.

That resolution flowed into other aspects of our relationship, including the allocation of responsibilities related to the management of our business.

An example of this occurred when we had to make the strategic business decision of how much presenting we would continue to do together versus how much our team of facilitators would take on. My objective was to have the highest-quality presentations possible out there, and my mistaken perception was that Mark wanted to mass-produce presentations to increase revenues. Because I had already learned from errors I had made in dealing with Mark, I was more prone to listen to his rationale and to give him leeway in orienting the direction of the company.

Had I not learned from past missteps, the talent that Mark had for building out a business would not have been realized. I would not have had the opportunity to write books and develop new business because of my acceptance of Mark's approach to growing the Institute and developing other strong program leaders.

The point is threefold. Good preparers keep on preparing; good preparers still make mistakes in both their preparation and execution; but good preparers use those mistakes as fodder for more preparation. The required midcourse adjustments do not mean you prepared poorly. They are inevitable. It simply stresses the importance of applying some of the same principles to midcourse adjustments and correcting mistakes as to prior preparation. Your mistakes are your best precedents.

I have found that the most successful professionals practice this sort of constant preparation. Willie Randolph, manager of the New York Mets, used multiple attempts to be named a big-league manager to improve himself for subsequent interviews, and to win one of the top jobs in baseball. Mayo Shattuck, the CEO of Constellation Energy, did not let his ego prevent him from making needed changes to a company strategy in the face of a firestorm of public opinion. From a failed program launch, Steve Mosko, president of Sony Pictures Television, learned how to reduce the risks of new shows in a whimsical and volatile industry. For each of these preparers, a mistake that requires an adjustment becomes a precedent for future preparation.

THE ADJUSTABLE MANAGER

 *Willie Randolph*

Willie Randolph does not like to lose. He is a natural-born competitor, be it in bowling with his buddies or managing a baseball team. He has won all his life, particularly as a star second baseman for the New York Yankees and later as one of Joe Torre's coaches for this New York dynasty. But for five or six years, he was struggling with a game at which he should have been winning—climbing the managerial ladder in Major League Baseball.

If you have ever repeatedly failed to achieve a prized objective, like winning a dream job, you'll find Willie's story helpful. Willie studied his repeatedly unsuccessful attempts to become a manager, and, by learning from his mistakes, he developed a preparation plan that led to the manager's job at the New York Mets.

Willie had his first interview in 1999. He had ten or eleven more over the next several years. He kept serving as a loyal and talented lieutenant to the Yankees' Joe Torre and kept wondering why the Reds, the Brewers, the Dodgers, the Phillies, then the Mariners, and even the Mets the first time around hired other managers.

Some sportswriters suggested that Willie was being interviewed so many times merely to enable teams to go through the motions of fulfilling commitments to consider minorities for managerial positions. Most of the interviews seemed formalities since the clubs had no intention of hiring Willie.

So here you are not only one of baseball's great players, but you have also paid the appropriate dues in the coaching ranks. And you feel trapped in a situation where you can't get what you want.

I had been Willie's agent for many years and suffered with him through the rejections. But after a few failures, I watched Willie turn each interview into an opportunity for preparation. I watched him get better and better at interviewing and at coaching in the meantime. Willie Randolph dedicated himself to learning from every interview and from his preparation for every interview. He was never a big power hitter as a player, but by the time the Mets hired him, Willie had gone from hitting singles and doubles in his interviews to nailing home runs on most questions.

"It got to be very difficult," Willie said. "There were interviews I went to that I knew going in I had no chance. A writer from Philadelphia who was a friend of mine told me that Larry Bowa had essentially been offered the job even before I interviewed. She encouraged me not to go. But I decided to go in there and try to knock their socks off. I just focused on what I could control, tried to leave them with a great impression when I walked out. I really turned every interview into a learning opportunity."

Willie tried to learn and improve in three ways: by identifying and formulating answers to questions he was repeatedly asked; by controlling his emotions and learning to provide a focused answer to the question; and by preparing through studying each team's players, staff, and younger talent. Each interview became an instructive precedent.

"I'll never forget in one of the early interviews they asked me, 'If you were a tree, what tree would you be?'" Willie said. "I was really taken aback at first. I didn't expect questions that tricky or philosophical. So I said something like a weeping willow. I swore if I ever saw that one again I would say a strong and stable oak. Another question that I wasn't ready for at first was 'How would you run spring training?' At first such a question threw me off guard. But then I went back to coaching at the Yankees and actually ran a spring training for Joe Torre. The next time I got the question, I had formulated my answer, had run one, and I hit it out of the park. The answer just flowed, and I think I even gave the interviewers a few insights into how to do it that they had not thought of or heard before. So interviewing became like baseball: the more you do something over and over, the better you get at it."

The second area in which Willie prepared anew had to do with the way he carried and conducted himself. Willie is a passionate competitor, and sometimes during the early interviews he let his passion carry his responses beyond the framework of the question.

I am grateful that Willie points to his attendance at one of our seminars at Shapiro Negotiations Institute as one turning point. Willie had been a baseball guy his whole life. He had not had much experience in the business world, and yet he was meeting with tried and tested businessmen at these job interviews. So at the seminar Willie got a sense of negotiating techniques and interactions that he kept discussing afterward. He became a student of negotiations and applied it to the next round of interviews after that season.

"I have a tendency to get passionate about what I am talking about," Willie said. "I learned to stick with the question and keep my answer to that small window. I also learned to ask questions back, to probe them for information, ideas, and opinions. I relaxed a bit, stepped back to focus on the question as opposed to how I would propose solving all their problems in one answer. I focused on pace and control in my response."

Willie also became a devoted note taker, and he would walk into his session with a notepad to take notes about the interview while it was occurring. And he also decided to walk into the interviews with some ideas laid out on his pad beforehand.

"I learned to have a list of things I wanted to hit on,"

Willie said. "As they asked me questions—sometimes ten guys would be firing questions at me—I would write down some of the questions and later analyze how I answered them. I figured I would see that question again down the road."

Third, Willie realized that it was critical to impress the club with his knowledge of their personnel. No one would expect as thorough and in-depth an analysis as Willie had developed, and it started to blow interviewers away.

"The preparation that you put into knowing their team signaled to them that you would really do the preparation required of a great coach," Willie said. "So I think that with each interview I learned how to structure my own preparation for that interview. It became much more organized and methodical."

Now, Willie keeps applying the lessons from those frustrating days. As a manager, a good part of his day is spent giving interviews to the plentiful New York press. And he also hires the coaches on his staff and plays a part in interviews in other areas of the organization.

"Those experiences helped me to be a better interviewer of my coaches," Willie said. "It prepared me for the press. I particularly learned how to lay out an answer in a clear and concise way. I learned from the process and keep applying the lessons to this day. I would do it all over again. I felt that way then and I feel that way now. It was all great preparation."

Willie kept refining his preparation techniques. He learned, adjusted, and got better and better while recognizing the value of the process. The result—manager of the New York Mets—was a product of treating a challenge as an opportunity to learn and to adjust accordingly.

DRAWING POSITIVE ENERGY
FROM MISTAKES

Mayo Shattuck

As a young investment banker in 1986, Mayo Shattuck made his name playing prominent roles in the initial public offerings of Microsoft, Oracle, Sun Microsystems, and Novell. More recently, as CEO of Constellation Energy, he saved his name and successfully steered his company by deftly adjusting to the public and political attacks on a proposed merger with Florida Power and Light amid ongoing rate hikes industrywide.

While controversial, the rate increases were largely a consequence of deregulation of the utility industry and increased fuel costs nationwide. But Mayo received blame for them, too. The manner in which Mayo dealt with this situation shows how important it is to recognize your mistakes and then recover from them by preparing to go in a new direction.

I know CEOs who are so self-certain that they refuse to even consider acknowledging mistakes and then preparing to take a new direction. There was, for example, a proposal for transforming the Maryland-based health insurer Care First from a nonprofit into a for-profit company. There was a public outcry, but instead of adjusting to the concerns that were raised, the leaders of Care First kept going full steam ahead. They not only lost their dream for the company, some also lost their jobs.

In contrast, Mayo admitted mistakes and terminated the

merger. He was self-confident enough to keep his ego from interfering with his need to adjust. As a result of the lessons he learned and the adjustments he made, Constellation's shareholder value has soared since the merger was ended.

Consolidation in the utility sector is a recent trend that made financial sense for the key players in the business. Onetime monopolies that were closely regulated by state agencies now had to compete in the open marketplace. But Constellation and Florida Power's timing was off. Opposition to consolidation was mounting. Energy prices were spiking after Katrina. Utility deregulation was leading to price increases in consumer rates. And, most important, a heated gubernatorial race was increasing tension in the Maryland legislature and making the merger a political plaything.

In short, the press tied a 72 percent increase in rates to the merger; political candidates tied their futures to stopping or supporting the merger; the state of Maryland fretted over the loss of a Fortune 500 company; and Mayo Shattuck found himself in the perfect storm.

"There was a lack of preparation on our part, or a lack of sensitivity to outside factors like politics and the media," Mayo said. "A lot of things can be assessed in a merger. The missing factor for us was how one of the topics would turn into both a media and political storm and have an effect on voters. We knew rates were going up, and we knew the election was coming. But we didn't tie those two variables together in the right way. They translated into wild voter dissent that politicians would react to by undermining the success of the deal. We didn't know how big the rate hike would be because when we announced the deal we had yet to go to auction to procure the power. Then the market started reacting to Katrina and we saw a severe spike in energy prices. We didn't connect these all together to get a comprehensive picture of the resistance. We relied on the traditional merger construct and didn't prepare for these variables."

But, rather than force the course, Mayo learned from his mistakes and adjusted in midcourse. Although he had prepared thoroughly to address the fear of losing a corporate headquarters in Baltimore (in fact, there was a probability that the new company's headquarters would be located in Baltimore five years after the merger), he shifted course to focus on serving the shareholders of Constellation once the merger seemed detrimental.

"We reassessed our real strategic options," Mayo said. "We analyzed our alternatives night and day for months trying to sort out a new direction. And we decided to terminate the deal. Our relations are almost as strong as ever with the principal legislators; shareholders are very happy; employees are still a bit unsettled but are coming around. It is true that all our preparation to deal with public sentiment was applied to the wrong issue. But we adjusted and I think the company will be better for the whole process."

Mayo's example is a reminder that the best leaders—be they CEOs or quarterbacks—don't get caught in the web of arrogance that keeps them from acknowledging mistakes. Rather, they draw on their experience; as part of their ongoing preparation, they make audible calls and adjustments to deal with unforeseen developments.

HOLLYWOOD LESSONS

Steve Mosko

With regard to preparation, Steve Mosko has almost every reason to be able to say: "Frankly, I don't give a damn."

As president of Sony Pictures Television, he sits in a huge Hollywood office in the mansion in which the last scene from *Gone with the Wind* was shot. Other luminaries who previously occupied it include Grant Tinker, Joe Kennedy, and Desi Arnaz.

Steve rose rapidly from radio sales on the East Coast to studio executive on the West. He negotiated the largest syndication of a program in television history—the multi-million-dollar, record-setting *Seinfeld* deal for Sony Pictures Television. He is as dashing as Clark Gable to boot. When Steve walks into a room in Hollywood, he gives you the sense that he was born to be there.

But the best of the naturals among us will admit that it does not come so naturally as it seems. Like all of us, Steve has made mistakes. The lesson he offers us is the way he uses those mistakes as precedents to better prepare for subsequent challenges.

Ironically, for a Hollywood guy, Steve is more influenced by sports than films.

"Sports taught me that no matter how well you practice, you still make mistakes in the game. The best learn from them—analyze them so that they almost subconsciously don't allow themselves to make the same mistake again."

It was Steve's high school football coach who best prepared him to make adjustments and learn from mistakes.

In one incident, Steve scored his first touchdown and acted like a hyperactive Terrell Owens during his celebration. Once he settled down and walked to the sidelines, his coach at John Carroll in northern Maryland grabbed him by the face mask and pulled his helmet so that they looked eye to eye.

"Act like you've been there before," Coach Gray said with a scowl.

Steve took the memory of that mistake with him to Hollywood.

"You walk into your first big meeting in Hollywood and you see people you have been reading about," Steve said. "For me, my preparation as an athlete was essential to making me feel more confident in my early days here. That mistake—my touchdown celebration—prepared me for my big meetings in a way I never imagined back then. But that is what great coaches, particularly at the high school level, are doing. They're preparing you and correcting mistakes in the hope that it has that long-term impact."

Steve became a Hollywood executive at a very young age. He especially impressed me with the way he realized that he still had a lot to learn even as his career took off. That openness to making adjustments and learning from mistakes has contributed significantly to Steve's progression and general competence. Two of his mistakes, one simple and one significant, demonstrate Steve's use of errors as opportunities to adjust his preparation.

The simple mistake is one anyone could make.

"In the early stages of the *Seinfeld* negotiations around the country, I made a simple but critical mistake," Steve said. "We were sending out our salespeople with an enormous amount of material for their presentations. Binders, videos, PowerPoint, materials. One day one of our guys checked it all in at the airport and the stuff never arrived in time for his presentation. This is a multimillion-dollar deal and we almost blew it. But we adjusted quickly. We perfected a system of FedExing and verifying arrival. We learned to package everything perfectly so that the materials would not be damaged. We even negotiated a good deal with FedEx. We sold *Seinfeld* in 213 markets and were negotiating with four to five stations in each market. We quickly learned that organization would alleviate the anxiety of our salespeople. That adjustment contributed in a mundane but significant way to our success."

Steve made the significant mistake in the late 1990s when Sony developed a new program that was billed as the way to attract the growing young urban audience in the late-night slot. A void for that audience had been created when Arsenio Hall ended his show. Steve had a dream partner in the legendary music producer Quincy Jones and his trend-setting magazine, *Vibe*. The combination of Quincy and Sony created great enthusiasm nationwide among local television stations' decision makers. They had the entertainer Sinbad as the host. But after the program's strong initial sales, the bottom fell out. Why?

"We made a huge mistake," Steve said. "Rather than have one producer running the show we ran it by committee. Everything from picking the host to designing the set, from deciding where we would shoot to setting a format, was made by group decision. Everyone was being so respectful to each other. We never had a strong point of view or someone leading the charge. We picked a young host who wasn't the greatest choice. Without a single clear vision, what could have been a major success got bogged down. An amazing idea got all fouled up. The program was off the air in a year."

Steve, who was executive vice president of sales at the time, got a valuable lesson in programming that he continues to apply as president of Sony Pictures Television today.

"You can only have one head coach per program," Steve said. "There has to be one person calling the shots and being held accountable. That is the only way I pursue programming ideas now. You can take ideas from many sources, but one executive producer has to make the decision."

Mundane or monumental, lessons like these can make the difference between someone who can adapt to situations or is overwhelmed by them.

Steve's matter-of-fact recognition that mistakes and adjustments are part of the preparation game is all too rare a thing for a top executive. But, like Mayo Shattuck or Willie Randolph, Steve's openness and willingness to adjust ensure that the same mistakes don't happen again.

Part 3

THE BENEFITS OF PREPARATION

Self-Confidence, Effectiveness, and Satisfaction

12

CONFIDENCE

HENRY V, SHAKESPEARE, AND CHURCHILL

Methodically prepared people not only achieve their objectives and perform at a higher level, they also have distinct levels of self-confidence, effectiveness, and satisfaction.

One of my favorite speechmakers is Shakespeare's Henry V. When actor Kenneth Branagh makes Henry's battle speech in his 1989 film version of the play—"Once more unto the breach, dear friends"—I can imagine the roar at the original Globe Theater back in Shakespeare's day. History's pundits would have it that Henry V was a playboy prince who, when the Crown beckoned, transformed himself into a great ruler and a fearless warrior overnight. Baloney!

Here's Winston Churchill, in his book *History of the English-Speaking Peoples*, setting the record straight:

> A gleam of splendour falls across the dark, troubled story of medieval England. . . . Henry V was King at twenty-six. The romantic stories of his riotous youth and sudden conversion to gravity and virtue when charged with supreme responsibility must not be pressed too far. If he had yielded to the vehement ebullitions of his nature this was no more than a pastime, for always since boyhood he had been held in the grasp of grave business.

That "grave business" is Churchillian rhetoric for something called preparation. Churchill tells us that, beyond the gallant confidence and eloquent bravado, Henry V was a master preparer. Churchill here states that victory at the Battle of Agincourt was more a result of methodical preparation than masterful rhetoric:

> During the whole of 1414 Henry V was absorbed in warlike preparation by land and sea. He reorganized the Fleet. Instead of mainly taking over and arming private ships, as was the custom, he . . . built many vessels for the Royal Navy. . . . The expeditionary army was picked and trained with special care. In spite of the more general resort to fighting on foot . . . six thou-

sand archers, of whom half were mounted infantry, were the bulk and staple of the army.

Henry V was no doubt a confident, dashing, and daring leader. But even in 1414, I'm sure it was preparation and not genetically granted or God-given poise that produced the resolute confidence that Branagh captured in the film.

I love to read history and biography to improve myself as a businessman and person. Abraham Lincoln and Teddy Roosevelt, like Henry V, were masters at using preparation to raise the possibility or even probability of succeeding. Each developed a thorough understanding of the people, circumstances, and facts of situations facing them. Each methodically analyzed challenges in a way that developed alternatives. Sure they came off as confident and charismatic, but the confidence they displayed was tied in large measure to the preparation they performed.

Despite his sometimes morose disposition, Lincoln embodied the old-school preparation ethic and remained steadfast during some of the darkest moments of any presidency in American history. You probably remember memorizing the Gettysburg Address in grade school. You probably remember the first time you visited the Lincoln Memorial in Washington, D.C.—and felt those wise eyes watching you as you read his great words inscribed on the walls.

How did Lincoln ever craft the eloquence and perfect pitch of the Address? How could Lincoln summon the confidence to deliver it at such a daunting moment in the young nation's history? By preparing in his devastatingly thorough way. Doris Kearns Goodwin, in *Team of Rivals: The Political*

Genius of Abraham Lincoln, details the preparation that Lincoln put in as a wordsmith.

> Books became his academy, his college. The printed word united his mind with the great minds of generations past. Relatives and neighbors recalled that he scoured the countryside for books and read every volume "he could lay his hands on." . . . He read and reread the Bible and Aesop's Fables so many times that years later he could recite whole passages and entire stories from memory. . . . Everywhere he went Lincoln carried a book with him. (p. 52)

Reading provided Lincoln with wisdom for writing and reaching his decisions. The precedents of history gave him the confidence he needed as a decision maker and writer.

Roosevelt had a famous swagger. But he prepared incessantly. For example, Edmund Morris notes in *Theodore Rex* that in 1903, in response to a request from the president of Columbia University for a list of recommended books, Roosevelt recollected the books he had read since taking office in 1901.

> It seemed like a strange request coming from the President of Columbia University, yet deserving of a full answer. He cast his mind back over what he had read since taking the oath of office, and began to scribble.
> Parts of Herodotus. The first and seventh books of Thuycidides; all of Polybius; a little of Plutarch; Aeschylus' Orestean trilogy; Sophocles' *Seven Against Thebes*;

Euripides' *Hippolytus* and *Bacchae;* and Aristophanes' *Frogs.* Parts of *The Politics of Aristotle* . . .

Morris adds several more books in Greek, and then another long list of books Roosevelt had read in French, as well as those he had "browsed if not deeply studied."

In my favorite example, Morris writes about how Roosevelt brilliantly prepared for his mediation of the Russo-Japanese War. He brokered the Treaty of Portsmouth in 1905 and won the Nobel Prize in 1906 for his efforts. To succeed, he acquired an unbelievable grasp of the history of the combatants; and he prepared for the negotiations by creating links with allies, building relationships within each combat sphere of influence, and analyzing alternatives with them. He defined each party's interests and set his strategy accordingly. He knew thoroughly that Japanese economic weakness drove their interest in peace. He understood the damage done to the Russian psyche and their expansionist plans by a series of stinging defeats by the Japanese. All this preparation gave him the confidence, that is, the swagger, to bully and broker the parties into peace.

I have always viewed the accomplishments and personas of Lincoln and Roosevelt with awe. But reading about them in the recent biographies humanizes them. And the books really drive home the link between their confidence and their preparation.

Sometimes seeing certain people and companies perform, I wonder if there is such a thing in any given field as a true natural who only needs minimal preparation to perform well. I used to think Lincoln and Roosevelt were naturals.

But the more I study them, I realize they were more like you and me. They needed to prepare.

Babe Ruth might be a mythic example, an extraordinary talent who, according to legend, likely had to prepare less than others. There is no denying the genetic and cultural advantages that certain people have. In business as in the arts or sports, you might find a person who makes it seem as if luck and genes have conspired to make preparation unnecessary.

But most naturals are made and not born. Be it Lincoln or Roosevelt, a confident athlete, doctor, politician, or confident-seeming company, methodical preparation plays an essential part in developing the self-confidence that plays so important a role in success.

SCENE: A BASEMENT IN MINNEAPOLIS, MIDWINTER

CAST: AN INVENTOR AND HIS SON

Joe Mauer

Joe Mauer, a quiet midwesterner, has become one of the best baseball players in the game and could someday be one of baseball's all-time greats. In 2006, *Sports Illustrated* put him on its cover below the headline, "American Idol." I laughed when I saw that cover: associating Joe with the television program of the same name plays into the notion of Joe as the natural. He isn't. He is another master preparer. Lots of talent. But first and foremost he is a preparer.

Joe is also one of the most quietly self-confident people I

have ever worked with. He exudes confidence—not in what he says but how he moves and acts. He walks up to the batter's box and it reminds me of watching him walk into a room; his confidence is almost tangible. But if you know Joe, you realize that most of his confidence results as much from his methodical preparation as from his bountiful talents. He is an incessant and methodical preparer as both a hitter and catcher.

I have known Joe well since he was in high school. The expectations have always been high for him. How many people get voted by *USA Today* as High School Baseball and Football Player of the Year in the same year? Had he not opted for baseball, he would have been the starting quarterback for the Florida State Seminoles.

His preparation ethic comes from his family. Joe's father, Jake, saw his son's talent and zeal for playing. But the cold Minnesota winters made baseball a daunting activity. So Joe's father analyzed the alternatives for his son's year-round development. He tried to find facilities large enough to allow for indoor batting practice. He looked for precedents of ballplayers from cold regions who succeeded despite the more limited practice opportunities. He researched how college programs in the North deal with the bad weather.

With no valid alternative at hand, Joe's father decided to invent a type of pitching device called Quick Swing, which deposits balls for batters to hit in confined areas like basements in Minnesota. It also allows hitters to practice the timing of a swing in a more precise way than other pitching machines.

"It, as you know, gets rather cold in Minnesota," Jake said. "And Joe loved to swing the bat. We don't have that big a basement, so I tried to concoct something that would allow Joe to keep practicing his swing all year long. Basically I built a tube that you feed a ball into and it accelerates very quickly as it comes down and drops in front of you. Joe and his brothers loved it."

Jake continued, "I think from an early age Joe was more confident than most kids because he simply practiced more. So when he was sixteen and playing on the 18 and Under USA team, he didn't seem nervous because so much repetition and practice made him sure of what he could do. Joe was never cocky, but he was confident beyond his years."

For hours each day Joe would work with his father perfecting his swing and, additionally, his understanding of the swing—its physics and mechanics, its flaws and strengths. This preparation refined Joe's talent. And, more important, the preparation gave him the confidence that comes from an effective method.

"If I know that I've done the necessary things to prepare for a game or even an at bat, then my confidence level rises and definitely improves my performance," Joe said. "You definitely have a greater confidence level going up against a pitcher or calling a game as a catcher when you have reviewed your notes on that pitcher or that team's hitters, when you have analyzed previous at bats and studied them over and over. I imagine entire games in my head before we play. I play out certain scenarios over and over so I can react when they happen. The preparation takes more time and energy, but it is all about gaining confidence."

Joe Mauer, though young as batting champions go, gained confidence of major-league proportions through preparation.

CONFIDENCE AS THE CLOCK TICKS ON A HOSTAGE'S LIFE

Gerald Brooks

You think Joe Mauer feels pressure when he is batting in the bottom of the ninth with the tying run on second, two outs, and a three-ball, two-strike count?

Imagine the pressure of facing life versus death: you're a hostage negotiator. Not like the guy in the movies who swaggers in, never sweats, and talks a potential murderer out of his rage with a few cool-as-a-cucumber chats on the cell phone.

Imagine the real thing: you arrive at a row house in which a fellow police officer is holding several people hostage. You don't know that he has already killed one of his hostages. You learn this in the middle of the negotiation just as you think you have established a rapport on the phone with him. Would the realization that you have developed an emotional connection with a murderer shake your confidence? You have to continue to give the suspect the feeling that you empathize with him despite the fact that you know he has blood on his hands.

It takes a lot of confidence to not lose your confidence when you get a midnegotiation jolt.

Or imagine you arrive at a farmhouse and a man is threatening to hang himself. Through your binoculars you see the rope with the noose hanging down from a beam. You also see empty liquor bottles scattered around the room. The suspect is demanding a bottle of whiskey or else he will hang himself. You know the first rule of negotiation is never to provide the suspect with alcohol. Suddenly he hangs up the phone, steps on a chair, and puts the noose around his neck.

Both of these events happened to Gerald M. Brooks, a police officer and member of the FBI's hostage task force. Without the preparation that gives him seamless confidence in his words, body language, tone of voice, and strategy, Gerald probably would have witnessed several more murders in the first case and a man hang himself in the second. Gerald believes that methodical preparation explains how he and his team convinced the police officer to surrender and how they rescued the drunken man just as he was about to take his own life.

"We were well into the conversation before I even knew what he had done," Gerald said of the negotiation with the police officer. "It can be a real blow to your confidence to find out something like that in the middle of a negotiation. But that circumstance had come up before in many of our mock exercises, so I was prepared for it. And I kept my focus on staying outside my role as a law enforcement officer and staying dedicated to providing a fellow human being with another day to live. In a funny way it takes real confidence in your preparation and approach to not judge anyone despite what you know they have done. My training gives me confidence that I won't make the worst mistake in my business—judging someone."

In the potential suicide, Gerald used his ability to identify interests to shift the topic of the conversation from suicide. He spent so much time talking with the man about the brands of different liquors and their different tastes that he bought time for a rescue squad to get into the house and snatch the man as he hanged himself.

Gerald focuses on two preparation principles to gain and maintain his unflappable confidence: scripting—rehearsing empathy in his daily relationships; and precedents—learning from previous hostage cases.

When he is negotiating, Gerald's primary strategy is conveying empathy. He must do it with sincerity, truly stepping out of his role as a police officer and shedding any moral position he may have with regard to what the hostage taker has done or threatens to do. Gerald needs complete confidence to be able to establish a relationship with a very confused and potentially dangerous individual. Preparation for this challenge is never ending. Gerald scripts empathetic statements in his head daily as he interacts with friends, family, and colleagues. The type of confidence he needs demands that he constantly be preparing. The collateral benefit to his family and friends is that Gerald must be the most empathetic person in their lives.

"I use every interaction in everyday life to practice my listening skills, my probing skills, and my ability to communicate clearly," Gerald said. "I always try to compliment people and offer positive critiques instead of criticisms. I need to find what people like and need and find the hook into their life and mind. This is not just something you turn on when the crisis hits. It's not like the movies where this natural negotiator walks in and saves the day. The preparation in real life is relentless."

In terms of learning from precedents, Gerald attends seminars around the country that are usually organized by police forces immediately after noteworthy hostage incidents.

"You start to develop a method based on all this study of other cases," Gerald said. "You have a checklist to assess the situation and the content and emotions of the person in this crisis. By studying each hostage event with colleagues, you establish a list of precedents so you go into the next negotiation with as much insight and confidence as possible."

Gerald, like Joe Mauer, develops his confidence by relying on a method. Whether for a ballplayer or a hostage negotiator, preparation fosters confidence.

CONFIDENT COMPANIES

Under Armour

Confident businesspeople are one thing. I see them all the time in my work. But over the years I've wondered whether there is such a thing as a confident company, a confident management team, a collectively confident group of people. The confidence of a leader can often rub off on a staff or team. But how does the whole become greater than the sum of its parts? My experience is that the best source of collective confidence is collective preparation.

Methodical preparation can cascade through the levels and divisions of a company or team. Sometimes skills of the best-prepared employee are simply imitated. This person can be the boss, a manager, a staffer, or a secretary. Sometimes team spirit makes preparation spread.

A preparation ethic can build internal momentum at a company so that individual preparation becomes a corporate methodology. It can become contagious to the point that it even becomes associated with the brand. Preparation itself can be marketed if the product is properly prepared.

That was the case with Under Armour, a company as confident as its name.

I have watched Under Armour grow from an idea in the head of founder and former college athlete Kevin Plank into a leader in performance apparel—clothing made for athletes and outdoors aficionados. Its marketing campaign sells confidence, and even associates the right apparel with confidence. You may be tempted to think Under Armour is as much a marketing juggernaut as a substantial company. After all, two of its commercials have become minor cultural phenomena. The first brought us the rallying cry, "Protect This House." The follow-up, which launched Under Armour's entry into the shoe market, delivered the catchy refrain, "Click-Clack."

But a look inside Under Armour reveals that preparation, not slick marketing, underlies that confidence. Research and development precede the image. Research and development give the company enough confidence to be brash in its marketing.

Under Armour has mastered the principle of defining interests. Customers' needs drive product development. Under Armour prepares by knowing its customer.

"We prepare a product for the market by asking a fundamental question: how does it help the athlete?" said Steve Battista, the head of marketing at Under Armour. "We build our brand by researching what athletes need, what innovation might help them. Then we start marketing by selling directly to them before we even advertise. Word starts to spread that the product works even before it becomes a brand."

Grassroots research among athletes from Little League to the big leagues, then, constitutes the foundation of Under Armour's preparation. Internally, Under Armour develops different designs that fit the criteria developed through their research. Chemists work on refining and advancing the product's materials. Veritable architects of apparel produce different designs that attempt to meet athletes' needs. And testing includes months of trials with potential customers whose feedback leads to still more refinement of the product.

The Click-Clack shoe launch is a case in point. I often have heard from athletes over the years that cleated shoes used in most sports are too heavy. Under Armour heard it, too, and set out to enter the market by leveraging these customers' interest. Its product development team designed a shoe, got feedback from athletes of all ages and talents, did extensive field testing, and adjusted the product according to the market's input. It stayed dedicated to the fundamental question: how do we make performance better?

The Click-Clack marketing campaign was also built on Under Armour research with focus groups. It made a connection with athletes by replicating the sound of cleats on concrete—the last sound they hear before stepping on the field. This seemingly small bit of preparation paid off: Under Armour captured a 20 percent market share of the cleats market sector in three months.

The commercial is catchy and clever. It presents very confident-looking athletes at the moment when their confidence must be at its greatest, their entrance into the arena.

As you walk the halls of Under Armour's headquarters, you feel a confidence among the employees. I have done corporate consulting for over thirty years, and I have been in many offices. But I have rarely felt such collective confidence as I do at Under Armour. When I talk with employees of all levels there, I notice that they are as eager to talk about their method of preparing a product as they are about their famed commercials. Under Armour is very clear about its objective of taking on the behemoth Nike in the sports apparel market. Its confidence in the face of such a challenge would seem farcical if Under Armour were a one-hit wonder with clever commercials. But a preparation principle—define the interests—gives credence to its confidence.

The confident company or team or university or firm or hospital, like the confident individual, more often than not prepares according to a set of clearly defined principles.

13

PREPARE AND CONQUER

A Mantra for Effective People

Revenue growth. Batting averages. Profit margins. Yards per game. Ratings. Five stars. Safety records. Election results. Investment returns. Applause. Cure rates. Cases won. Tickets sold. High fives.

Like preparation, it is hard to define effectiveness, but there are plenty of ways to measure it. All these measurements and statistics, however, can overwhelm and even deceive.

I prefer to define effectiveness in terms of preparation: did your results fulfill your objectives?

There are people whose effectiveness is almost tangible or visible. You feel it when you are working with them. You feel it when you are around them.

I have noticed that many effective people embrace the process as much as the result. Measurements of success are great, but they do not seduce many effective people. The profilees who fill this book almost unanimously take as much satisfaction in the process of preparing as in the result. That, I think, is what really helps make them effective. Talent, charisma, and sheer energy all help. But people devoted to a process are usually people who achieve results.

In this chapter, you read about two people who are unusually effective. Shirley Franklin is the mayor of a sprawling city, and Don Cohan is a real estate developer who has defeated two cases of devastating cancer. Their effectiveness is so bound up with their preparation that it is difficult to determine where their preparation stops and execution begins. For them, preparation and execution blur together. So do method and instinct. And their effectiveness usually blends from work into life.

GOVERNING EFFECTIVELY

Mayor Shirley Franklin

I bet that many of the citizens of Atlanta, Georgia, know that Mayor Shirley Franklin, whom *Time* magazine called one of the top five mayors in America, is uncommonly effective. What they may not realize is how much she relies on methodical preparation as the key to her effectiveness as a leader.

Shirley has been in politics long enough to know that preparation alone does not guarantee effectiveness. Politics, bureaucracies, cities themselves are too unruly. But Shirley realizes fully that methodical preparation lets her control the only variables that she can: herself and her office. Her objective is to be as prepared, and consequently as effective, as she can be. The rest will take care of itself.

Shirley had two effective preparation mentors: Andrew Young and Maynard Jackson. She was city manager in Atlanta when each man was mayor there.

"They gave me the latitude to develop my leadership skills," Franklin said. "I started as the commissioner of cultural affairs with a budget of $5 million and a staff of less than thirty. By the time I left government in 1990 I was managing over eight thousand people and a budget of several billion dollars. Andy and Maynard allowed me to grow as a manager of people and issues."

Indeed, Shirley credits both mentors with her personal development as much as her professional growth. They identified her skills and helped prepare her. She had conversations with each previous mayor about their mistakes, their successes, and their approach to leadership. They willingly served her as precedents.

"Andy used to say that he preferred a no-fault analysis of problems," Franklin said. "It is not about blaming people for a problem but finding the solution, then learning and improving if there was a mistake."

But the greatest precedent that her mentors may have provided Shirley is their approach to the transitioning from campaigning to governing. Franklin had worked on campaigns and in various government offices since she was a teenager, but she had never run for office.

"Both men saw the potential in me to make the transition,"

Shirley observed. "But it was our preparation together that really helped educate me about campaigns. And they helped guide me from the electoral process to governing with their own insights and lessons."

Shirley directly ties her effectiveness in making the transition to her preparation for it. She gives the impression of an effective city manager as much as an elected mayor. And that, I think, is a big part of the reason for her success.

From her work as a city manager, Shirley learned that there is a direct relationship between preparation and effectiveness and between effectiveness and reputation. And so it was almost a natural decision for her to tackle Atlanta's decaying water and sewer infrastructure as one of her major initiatives as mayor.

I was once in Jerusalem with Baltimore mayor Kurt Schmoke. We were chatting with Teddy Kollek, the mayor of that ancient city. These two gentlemen lived thousands of miles apart and were dealing with very different issues as mayors. They had every reason to struggle to find common ground for a conversation. But somehow they immediately started talking about sewers and potholes. They entered right into the nitty-gritty of each other's worlds. And they were both lamenting the awesome challenge of trying to adequately maintain the infrastructure of their cities.

So I recalled that conversation when I discussed with Shirley why she would pick infrastructure as a top item on her agenda as mayor. Homelessness, affordable housing, even crime—so many challenging issues somehow seem less daunting and more exciting than tackling the multibillion-dollar task of rehabilitating miles of pipes and tubes.

"I doubt anyone ever heard of a political candidate saying

that if I'm elected I'm going to tear up your city and repair the sewers," Shirley said. "But this was a fundamental issue related to watershed infrastructure and affected the sanitation and our drinking water, too."

So Shirley, with her effectiveness on a basic issue, achieved two objectives: she won the confidence of her constituency and set a tone for preparation in her administration. That tone was set with a strategy that we see far too little in elected office: address the basic issues and not necessarily the attention getters.

Shirley prepared for the infrastructure project according to her trusted method: assembling experts on a critical topic from outside the city. Her objective was clear: fix the problem as quickly and cost-effectively as possible. And so she picked her team according to their talents and the demands of the topic.

She summoned environmental experts, engineers, land use lawyers, and water specialists from outside of Atlanta. She wanted an unbiased education from people who had no financial or personal stake in the matter. She does this for every big topic she tackles. She assembles precedents, develops her objectives, and executes her strategy based on what she and her team learn.

"Based on their advice we learned the issues and developed a plan, but also broadened the consensus on the matter," Shirley said. "The neutrality of the experts helps my constituency trust in the strategy. But they also see how we are really preparing to find the right solution."

The preparation that goes into such an assembly of experts requires a lot of effort—probably more effort than many local elected officials are willing to exert. But Shirley is again merely trying to control all the variables she can control. The development of an informed and expert policy is the first step in remedying any civic crisis. Effectiveness is so much easier to achieve when the mayor and her staff are confident about their policy and satisfied that they have prepared properly.

Shirley, who laughs about her early days as a public speaker, admits that she was ineffective and poorly prepared.

"People in my office used to cringe when I stood up to speak," she said. "I was particularly poor at extemporaneous speaking."

So the mayor decided to prepare to be extemporaneous. She studied other great speakers, including her two mentors, on tape. She listened more closely when attending events at which others spoke well. She became a collector of great speeches.

But she also started to script.

Shirley gave one of the best of many speeches at the funeral for Coretta Scott King, the wife of Martin Luther King Jr. It lasted four minutes.

"But I prepared and rehearsed for probably fifteen hours," the mayor said.

Now Shirley scripts for speeches, meetings, and one-on-one encounters. Her scripting raises the image of preparedness that she conveys. And you can ask her staff members who used to cringe about her increased effectiveness on the stump. The visibility and accessibility of her preparation is a quality I see in the people profiled in this book. Their effectiveness as leaders—of a unique school or of a city, of a company or a television studio—is tied to the transparency

and contagiousness of their devotion to methodical preparation. They cherish process as much as success. Like Shirley,
they know that a process likely leads to success.

PREPARING TO SURVIVE

Don Cohan

You probably know someone who has had cancer. So you
also know how difficult it can be to work your way through
the daunting bureaucracy of medicine in America. Surviving
a lethal cancer takes guts and a few breaks. It also demands a
focused preparation for how to steer through an overwhelming system of doctors, tests, opinions, and delays. A systematic approach to preparing for treatment is the only effective
way to deal with both a deadly disease and a mind-boggling
hospital and insurance system, but too few people use one.

My stepbrother, Don Cohan, was a solid preparer all his
life. His commitment to preparation won him innumerable
medals in sailing, including a bronze in the 1972 Olympics.
It helped him build a real estate business that gave him
enough material success to fund a dormitory at his alma
mater, Amherst College.

But ultimately, Don demonstrated the effectiveness that
methodical preparation can bring you when he survived two
separate battles with one of the worst types of cancer, a
dreaded "4b" Hodgkin's lymphoma.

Don's objective was obviously to survive and continue to
spend as much time as possible with his beloved family.
He methodically researched treatment centers, modes of
treatment, physicians, mental and physical therapies, and

engaged in just about every principle of preparation. He found precedents—not many, but enough to raise his confidence—of people who had survived his type of cancer. He canvassed his contacts and scoured the media and medical journals for alternatives. He identified and examined each possible alternative and hospital for treatment. He set a strategy based on identifying great doctors who would let Don make the decision to undergo treatments considered too grueling for someone his age.

His greatest talent as a preparer was revealed in how he assembled his team. He interviewed doctors, he went to a psychiatrist to shift his grief and fear onto a third party away from his family, and he designated his very capable wife, Trina, as the deputy in his battle.

"I said to myself, 'Don, you may be very good in your line of business, but you know nothing about this one'," Don said. "So I assembled this team and defined a role for each person on that team and narrowed my life to them and them only during that time. My strategy was to use my team to enable me to beat this thing."

The confidence and effectiveness of Don's family team rubbed off on his doctors. Because of my experiences with doctors and hospitals as an adviser and board member, I am firmly convinced that doctors sense the preparedness of a patient and a family team and respond to it. It is only human nature to raise your game to the level of the people you are interacting with.

Imagine how a doctor would respond if you as the patient walked in and courteously presented a preparation checklist to review together. That is essentially what Don did, and

I am certain he achieved an attentiveness and level of collaboration from his doctors because of it.

Every morning Trina would put a list on the bathroom mirror of his medications and visits for the day. One morning Don was so sick that he just sat vomiting into the toilet bowl. Trina came in and was startled to find Don laughing almost hysterically all the while he had his head in the toilet.

"She asked me why I was laughing," Don said. "I gargled out the line that everyone who ever thinks they are a big shot ends up with their head in a toilet bowl."

But the ability to laugh, I think, somehow came from Don's preparation for the fight. He was laughing at himself, maybe even laughing at the devil. But the very ability to do so had to emanate from a confidence that he had prepared for this biggest challenge as methodically as he could. He had done all he could do to be effective. A good result would be gravy. And, in a funny way, his reflexive commitment to a preparation process distracted him from thoughts of death. The process became his fixation instead of his demise.

Donald's example taught me that something as mundane as a preparation checklist can be applied even to the challenges of serious illness. He knew he had done all that he could do in terms of preparing to be effective. He knew he had used preparation, like Mayor Franklin, to control all the variables that he could. This thorough preparation—this certainty that he had done all he could do to be effective—gave him the freedom to greet the absurdity of his situation eye to eye beside the toilet bowl.

Methodical preparation helps keep Don alive and effective to this day.

14

YOU CAN GET SOME SATISFACTION

My friends, novelists Jim and Karen Shepard, say that preparation is all about "rigor and optimism." It is rigorous to do, but gives you optimism about your project or performance that is a direct result of the systematic work that went into it.

And just as methodical preparation instills confidence and makes you more effective, it can also provide a strong sense of satisfaction.

A funny thing happened to me after we developed and started teaching the preparation checklist at our consulting firm. I realized I could utilize many of its principles as guidelines in most aspects of my life. I realized that it brought rigor and optimism to almost anything I did.

The concepts of a preparation checklist—its methodical logic and flow—became a part of many challenges I undertook. And, just as this increased my performance at work, it increased my satisfaction away from work. My life's interactions took on a new clarity and focus.

You can get so wrapped up in things that you lose effectiveness. And you can forget about the point of it all: satisfaction. During the 2006 Winter Olympics in Torino, Italy, I heard an interview with an Olympic figure skater who said she had overprepared. You hear this often with regard to performance in sports or the arts. People say: "I'm not sharp"; "I overprepared"; "I thought too much." Such words are usually uttered by people who don't look at preparation as a satisfying process. They only look to it as a way to produce results.

After years of preparing to produce results, I have lately started to enjoy the process of preparation. This is something like the old lines "art for art's sake" or "the journey is the destination." Preparation for preparation's sake; the method becomes as much, or almost as much, the point of it all as the result.

CRAZY FINGERS

 *Ben Carson*

Ben Carson, the famous pediatric neurosurgeon, is a good example of someone who takes deep satisfaction in the process of preparation. He loves his work—saving and transforming the lives of children. But I think his passion for his work also comes from his complete dependence on and enjoyment of methodical preparation. Ben gets his greatest satisfaction in life from helping people. But he also finds significant satisfaction in the sheer process of being a surgeon and administrator. Preparation for Ben borders on ritual: he goes through his day exuding tranquility because he is so focused on his daily method.

"I take great pleasure in preparation," Ben said. "It gives me serenity. In my line of work I have a real responsibility to avail myself of as much information as I can and to learn from the things other physicians have done. I need check-lists and structure to step from one patient to the other. If you are prepared, the likelihood of success is that much greater. And if you are well prepared and still unsuccessful, you can live better with yourself."

Ben overcame severe economic disadvantage to achieve his success. He has an extraordinary mind and uncannily deft fingers: these were as much God-given skills as Joe Mauer's vision or hand-eye coordination. But like Mauer, Ben harnesses his skills with an insistently methodical approach. Because of his impoverished background, he was driven to succeed partly because he always wanted to overcome the feeling that he was never as good as the other guy.

As a kid living in the inner city of Detroit, Ben seemed to be impeded from moving ahead in the world by the poverty that plagued his neighborhood. But his mother prepared him continually; she had him learn to play classical music and read great books. A funny thing happened one day when I was speaking with Ben in his office. The only interruption was a call from his wife. She told him that at that instant there was a piece of lovely music on the local classical music station and that he should turn it on. Ben folded his surgeon's hands together and his fingers in that moment looked like those of a piano player.

"If I don't feel prepared going into a surgery, then I don't feel comfortable," Ben said. "And if I don't feel comfortable, I don't do it. I have elected to not do surgeries when I didn't feel completely prepared. My recognition is that preparation for anything—especially for surgery—came from the way my mother taught me to improve my reading skills. She would come home at night after working in the homes of wealthy people and try to get me to spend as much time reading as they did. We worked on spelling and syntax and grammar. Her method of teaching me really reinforced that you need a step-by-step approach to almost anything you do. And I realized that reading really prepares you for anything because it helps you use your imagination to create a picture of what you are reading or, in the case of preparation, what you are about to do."

I don't know a more driven man on this earth: Ben wants to heal the world. And every night he goes to bed picturing in his head how to do it the next day—running through his checklist for surgery, envisioning his patients and their families, visualizing and double-checking. And Ben's serenity makes me guess that he sleeps well, too. Preparation gives him a satisfaction that approximates the joy he takes from healing and saving lives. And his joy is a contagious thing, as many of his patients testify.

THE PIANO MAN

Leon Fleisher

Piano virtuoso Leon Fleisher illustrates the link between preparation and satisfaction as much as anyone I know. I first met Leon in the midst of a potentially crippling strike of the Baltimore Symphony Orchestra. It was prior to the opening of their new symphony hall, and I was asked to mediate between management and the players. Federal mediators and other civic leaders had failed to bring a resolution.

As I prepared and probed my way through the positions of the parties, I asked Leon to help educate me in the politics and practicalities of professional music because he was held in highest esteem by all sides. Leon helped me define the interests of management and of the musicians; he helped me understand the alternatives each side faced in their lives; he taught me how orchestras pick their teams and how management and boards do, too. I shared my proposed scripts with Leon to get his reaction and suggestions before I met with the union and management. When the strike was settled one morning at 5 A.M., the first person I decided to wake up with the news was Leon.

I think of the line by the poet Robert Browning—"a man's reach should exceed his grasp . . ." I came to realize that Leon, in his music, was reaching for something few of us contemplate in our work. When he played the piano with those two God-given hands, Leon was reaching for a sort of heaven. Call it ecstasy, joy, or merely contentment; Leon likes to say that there is an "inevitability to a great piece of music." He helped me understand that that "inevitability" might be what we call bliss.

So imagine depending on your work for that sort of thing. Pretty high stakes, but lots of satisfaction. And then imagine what Leon went through: he suffered the loss of the ability to play the piano with his right hand. Speaking of grasping, he could not even give a firm handshake. Forget about livelihood and fame and history. In 1964, an unidentifiable disease robbed Leon of his ability to reach for what he longed for whenever he sat down at his instrument. The child prodigy who studied with the maestro Artur Schnabel from age nine to nineteen could no longer play the piano.

"The piano for me is not an instrument but an extension of myself," Leon said. "It is not a foreign object. The keys are continuation of the fingers."

So part of his body had been ripped away. Leon could not turn to his awesome talent to get him through, so instead he turned to preparation. He redefined the objectives of his life, and he analyzed the precedents and alternatives that could see him through his struggle.

"I went from one therapy to another," Leon said. "I decided to seek out every alternative that I could. There was also a body of work for left-handed playing, but I denied that for several years. That would have been an admission that I couldn't play."

Then one day Leon finally decided to continue his pursuit of innovative treatments while redefining his relationship with music. He analyzed his objectives and found that he could achieve in the role of teacher some of the satisfaction and joy that he saw his mentor Artur Schnabel feel as he taught a handful of gifted students in his tiny apartment with two pianos on Central Park West in New York. Leon also turned to conducting, which allowed him to share the movements of music with fine orchestras.

Leon used the precedent of his famous teacher and the alternative of conducting to restore his satisfying relationship with music. And he at last dedicated himself to playing compositions for the left hand. Though not as satisfying as using two, the left-handed playing brought Leon that longed-for bliss during what he calls, "certain phrases every now and then." His process of repreparation as a musician drew on the same sort of checklist that he and I used to analyze the parties and potential for a settlement of the symphony strike.

Leon did get a reprieve. As a result of surgery for carpal tunnel syndrome (due to his clutching the baton while conducting), Leon regained the use of his right hand in late 1981. But the gods teased Leon a bit. I attended his great return to two hands—he played with two hands at the inaugural concert of the new symphony hall in an event that achieved front-page coverage from the *New York Times*. But well before the performance, he knew things still weren't right. The keys weren't an extension of the fingers of his right hand. He could manipulate them, move across them in a way his hand had not been able to do for years. But the piano wasn't one with him. Leon was despondent. He accused himself of "deception." He went on with the show as a good showman is called to do. But that night, in front of a concert hall filled with both classical music lovers and people longing to see the comeback kid, Leon felt no bliss. He felt disdain for himself.

"Then a funny thing happened once I acknowledged publicly that I wasn't cured," Leon said. "There had been ten big concerts scheduled. I expected them all to cancel, because they were premised on a falsehood of my playing with two hands. But only one canceled." So Leon continued to perform with the left hand and continued in his roles as teacher and conductor.

Then one day in 1995 he got a call from one of the experts on the diverse medical team he had assembled as part of his preparation. Dr. Daniel Drachman of the Johns Hopkins Medical School recommended that Leon try a Botox-based therapy that the National Institutes of Health in Washington, D.C., was running as a trial.

The therapy started to work, and everyone suddenly realized that all those muscular and nerve and skeletal treatments were misguided. Leon suffered from a brain-based disorder called focal dystonia. And the neurological messages sent from his brain to cause his fingers to curl involuntarily could be short-circuited by the Botox to allow him to play without his fingers curling. He was not cured, but his condition was improved enough to begin playing again on occasion with two hands.

The show went on because of the new treatment and in spite of Leon's sense of self-deception. And it goes on to this day, with Leon still conducting around the world and teaching a group of students at the Peabody Conservatory. His persistent preparation as a patient mirrored his preparation as a musician. Leon never gave in because he realized that preparation as a teacher or conductor could give him the satisfaction he needed to keep going. This newfound satisfaction gave him the strength he needed for his constant preparation as a patient.

In an era of emoting and gesticulating virtuosos, Leon remains pianissimo. I don't know much about classical music, but I know fortissimo, "loud," and I know pianissimo, or "softly." Leon is a soft player. In fact, he stands out for his softness even to the top classical music critics. It is his signature as a piano player and conductor.

Leon set about changing career tracks, identifying new challenges, and seeking bliss in new ways. He prepared himself pianissimo but full bore. He dared to prepare for a new way of life and found his old satisfaction because of diligent preparation.

"The discipline of preparation enables you to deliver up to at least 80 percent of your best when under the pressure of performance," Leon said.

Under pressure for so many years, Leon keeps delivering.

In December of 2007, Leon, along with Martin Scorsese, Diana Ross, and other luminaries, were named Kennedy Center Honorees. Earlier in that year, a documentary about Leon was nominated for an Academy Award. He walked down the red carpet alongside the stars. Called *Two Hands*, the movie is a testimony as much to Leon's repreparation as to his talent.

Today, when Leon shakes your hand, he grasps it. He reaches out with gusto when he meets you, and as he holds your hand two of his fingers curl under. He is seventy-nine years old, still reaching for a new way of life while holding on to an old one. He is still preparing for the complete recovery of the use of his right hand even as he prepares his students and orchestras for music's bliss. But more than ever he is a satisfied musician.

Something as simple as the preparation principles can help you achieve something as monumental as Leon's comeback. Preparation was his antidote to despair. Leon has come to seek a new form of satisfaction. Being a prodigy or a maestro is now secondary to preparing other musicians and preparing himself to play in a new way.

The sheer act of preparing—for a speech, a presentation, a negotiation, or a team meeting—has brought me moments of amazing satisfaction, too. I am not a world-class musician who is blessed enough to find bliss in a string of sounds. But I share with Leon and many others the conviction that preparation is a craft. And I am a methodical preparer who at times blissfully loses himself in preparation. It is amazing what you can discover when you dare to prepare.

APPENDIX

The Preparation Principles Checklist

CHALLENGES YOU FACE	
SITUATION SUMMARY	
OBJECTIVES Define your goals. What would you like to accomplish in this transaction or in dealing with this challenge?	

PRECEDENTS Transactions or experiences that can influence the outcome or provide a model for guidance. What have you or others done to deal with similar situations? What are some examples of results from those situations?	
ALTERNATIVES What are the various outcomes you want to consider? To what degree do they satisfy your objectives? What could happen if things don't work out? What are their options if the other party chooses not to work it out with you?	
INTERESTS What objectives or desires does the other side have beyond their stated positions? What do they want—need—that you might be able to address?	

STRATEGY/NEXT STEPS What is your plan? What steps does it involve? When and how will you probe?	
TIMELINE Lay out the time period during which you want to accomplish your objectives. When can you be expected to accomplish what steps in the process outlined in your strategy?	
TEAM Are you doing this alone or with others? What's everyone's role? What do you know about the other side's participants? Biographical information? Authority? Their personalities?	

| **SCRIPT** Write out the message or proposal you want to make. Include probing questions and hypotheticals. Share it with a team member or associate acting as your devil's advocate. Once you are satisfied, build confidence in delivering the hard message with practice. | |

This form provides a format for organizing ideas to help you set a strategy for challenges and transactions in your life. It is not intended that you fill in this form with every piece of information at your disposal. Instead, provide bullet points that will enable you to talk more efficiently with others when discussing the situation. You should not feel as if you need to write a complete answer on the checklist itself, but you should be able to provide that answer when asked questions generated from someone's review of the bullet points on your planner checklist.

ACKNOWLEDGMENTS

This book presents my core convictions on the subjects of preparation, success, and satisfaction. But it represents much more because it is also the product of friendships and partnerships that shaped and informed it.

I will never forget the many moments Greg Jordan and I shared—exhilaration after sharing a meal or a meeting with some of our subjects, intense meetings and e-mail exchanges, and a joy in words. Greg understood my passion for preparation and was unceasing in challenging me to articulate it in a manner that I hoped would inspire others.

Over the years, our team at the Shapiro Negotiations Institute helped construct the foundation of the preparation principles, and their input and research during the writing of this book helped make it far better. Mark Jankowski, Todd Lenhart, John Buelow, and Michael Blackstone gave us transforming suggestions. And our interns, Kate Maas, Cristina Maas, Ian Greenberg, and Jack Bisciotti were unstinting in their research assistance. Kim Talbott gave us an extra measure of devotion and help, and made this project better for her involvement.

The thirty-eight people who graciously allowed us to profile them became the backbone of this book. We left each meeting amazed at their talents and passion for proper preparation. They also risked our conveying their thoughts accurately and effectively, and I thank them for their trust as well as time.

Our readers challenged us to enliven the notion of preparation: Joann Davis, who not only gave her invaluable insights, but also shared the thoughts of her husband, Kenneth Davis, who helped create the title; Mike O'Pecko, who read each draft as if it were his own; Greg's parents, Tom and Ginger Jordan, who demonstrated where their son got his writing genes.

Along the way, friends such as Michael Maas, Dennis Mannion, Jennifer Gately, my assistant, Gloria Dausch, and my son, David Shapiro, contributed significantly as well. And my thanks go to my agent, David Black, for always being there, and for his sage advice and support.

I appreciate being challenged to be better, and that's what our editor, John Mahaney, did throughout this process. I may have thought we were finished at several points, but John's insights and questions kept coming. He never ceased in his pursuit of a better work.

Finally, my ultimate editor/adviser is my wife, Kathryn Adams Shapiro. She writes better and sees more than I do, and uses those talents to help make me achieve my objectives. And I love her deeply as she helps me PREPARE for all that life brings.

INDEX

ABOUT THE AUTHORS

Ronald M. Shapiro has had a rich and varied career as a civil rights and corporate lawyer, sports agent, entrepreneur, and business executive. He is the cofounder of the Shapiro Negotiations Institute, which has trained more than 250,000 people in the art of negotiation, in dealing with difficult people, and in learning the skill of being a great listener. He has not only represented Hall of Fame players such as Cal Ripken Jr. and Kirby Puckett but has advised an array of corporate and political leaders, helped settle a major symphony orchestra strike, diffused racial tension in a metropolitan police department, and helped find solutions to Major League Baseball's owner-player and umpire conflicts.

Gregory Jordan is a freelance writer whose articles have appeared in the *New York Times*, *The Hill*, beliefnet.com, and *Crisis* magazine.

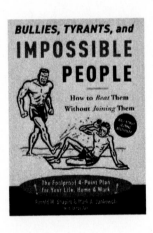